First Orthodox
Presbyterian Church
Sunnyvale, CA

# THE MEASURE OF GREATNESS

Other books by Hugh Steven:

Manuel
Night of the Long Knives
You Eat Bananas
Miracles in Mexico (Hefley/Steven)
The Reproducers
It Takes Time to Love
Kim
They Dared to be Different

# THE MEASURE OF GREATNESS

## HUGH STEVEN

Scripture quotations in this volume are from the
King James Version of the Bible.

First Printing, 1973
Second Printing, 1976

*Library of Congress Cataloging in Publication Data*

Steven, Hugh
  The measure of greatness.

  1. Missions – New Guinea.    2. Steinkraus,
Walter.    3. Steinkraus, LaVonne.    I. Title.
BV3680.N52S88        266'.023'0922 [B]        73-14950
ISBN 0-8007-0634-X

# *Contents*

# *Preface*

I was using the Xerox copying machine when Dr. Benjamin Elson, Wycliffe's executive director, asked soberly if I had heard about the Steinkraus family.

"No," I said, trying to extract their faces from the many hundreds of my Wycliffe colleagues.

"They were all buried in a landslide," he said. "I am just now advising their next of kin. Will you write up something about them?"

I felt weak and sick inside. I said I would and in a few moments he returned with a brown file folder. The tab read: Steinkraus, Mr. and Mrs.

I began at the front. The last communiqué was a yellow Western Union telegram from the New Guinea director.

MARCH 21/71   URGENT   WALT AND VONNIE STEINKRAUS AND CHILDREN BURIED IN VILLAGE BY LANDSLIDE SUNDAY 21ST STOP PLEASE NOTIFY NEXT OF KIN VONNIE'S FATHER HAS HEART CONDITION   PENCE

I flipped to the back and found another Western Union telegram, white and faded.

NOVEMBER 5/54   FEEL REASONABLY SURE BOARD WILL ACCEPT VONNIE   NYMAN

I then scanned the material in between and subsequent letters and diaries that were in safekeeping at the New

Guinea base and found a story of common people with uncommon courage, devotion, and simplicity.

I saw a cute little nurse laughing and riding bareback across Wisconsin's dairy land. I saw a young man in the extremity of heartache write, "Things we can't understand belong to Him."

I saw the measure of greatness in two people who were reaching out for the important additions to their faith that Peter talks about in his second Book, starting at the first chapter, verse five. I saw the measure of greatness—two people who willingly let God have His way with them when life was easy and happy, and when it didn't make sense.

Lewis Carroll used a rabbit's hole to get his readers into a different world so they could see themselves in a non-threatening way. Authors before and since have used a variety of techniques to turn their readers around to see a more complete view. C. S. Lewis used a bus in *The Great Divorce*. Jonathan Swift used six-inch Lilliputians to expose the stuffy bureaucracy of his day. And sometimes God uses death as a vehicle to turn us around so we can see life from His point of view.

But this book is more about life than death. It's the story of greatness in two people, expressed in their love of life, nature, their chosen profession, each other, and God.

It is the story of two lives that are, in my judgment, the perfect example of Christ's words, ". . . the last shall be first, and the first last" (Matthew 20:16). And that the measure of greatness in a man is not judged by his looks or height, but by his thoughts and intentions (*see* 1 Samuel 16:7).

—HUGH STEVEN

# In Appreciation

With extraordinary fidelity, Walt and Vonnie Steinkraus preserved a lifetime of detailed records, diaries, and personal correspondence. These were carefully gathered together by their New Guinea colleagues. I express my deep appreciation to Wycliffe's New Guinea branch for insight and care in handling these materials and sending them to me—and for their help and hospitality during my recent visit.

I would like to express special appreciation to Vonnie's parents, Mr. and Mrs. Arthur Schreurs, and her sister, Phyllis Meier. Though it was painful, and at times tearful for them, they provided personal memories and anecdotes valuable to the writing of this book.

To Walt's sisters—Edna, Marge, and Violet; to his brothers, Sam and Willy. To Gil Dodds, Winnie Christensen, Ellis Mooney, Jim Dean, Alan Healey, Al Pence, and a host of people too numerous to list who supplied important supplementary material. And my apologies to the many close friends of Walt and Vonnie who wrote meaningful reflections which for reasons of duplication and limit of book length, were not used.

Finally, to my wife, Norma, who with more than unusual patience organized and cataloged the great volume of letters, reports, and diaries. And who, more than I, is responsible for the chapter on reflections. I thank her also for her efficient editing and typing of the final manuscript.

Above all I praise God who gave me the privilege of writing this story, and who taught me much about His sovereignty and the meaning of true greatness.

# 1 The Measure of Greatness

Walter Steinkraus sent two letters, a month apart, to Wycliffe Bible Translators' home office in Glendale, California. The first, sent from Lombard, Illinois, was dated November 1, 1956.

> Miss LaVonne Schreurs and I became acquainted at Norman, Oklahoma, during the summer of 1955 and since then have considered marriage. I am looking forward to service in New Guinea and I am grateful to the Lord for leading me in this direction. LaVonne has also expressed her desire to transfer from Peru to New Guinea. If this is permitted, we would like to express a state of engagement. A refusal by you will be cheerfully accepted as the Lord's leading.
>
> Sincerely,
>
> *Walter Steinkraus*

The Board's answer came a month later, on December 3, and read in part,

> . . . Since Miss Schreurs has been in Peru for less than a year, the Board feels her early return to the United

States might cause public misunderstanding at home. We also feel her premature leave would cause extra burdens on Peru's medical program since a nurse replacement could not arrive for several months . . . .

The Board assured Walt this was not final. They would discuss it further when they heard from their field directors. The letter then ended with a casual suggestion that Walt might consider changing his assignment from the South Pacific to Peru.

Four months earlier Walt had received his assignment to the South Pacific area during his final summer of Wycliffe's linguistic training at Norman, Oklahoma. For Walt this assignment was the happy fulfillment of a hard twenty-year goal. His answer to the Board was swift and concise:

. . . Thank you kindly for informing me of your deliberations regarding LaVonne Schreurs and me. From the beginning we have committed this to the Lord and continue to trust He will direct you in the final decision.

These are my feelings regarding the possibility of having my assignment changed to Peru. I have no desire to go to Peru. I would rather go to New Guinea single if LaVonne's transfer is not to be, for I feel more and more that this is the Lord's place for me. I believe He has prepared me for this letter. Just yesterday, the day your letter arrived, there was a marked deepening of my burden for the tribes of New Guinea.

As I wrote before, whether LaVonne is permitted to transfer or not, the Board's decision will be cheerfully accepted as His leading.

Sincerely yours,

*Walter Steinkraus*

To the "enlightened" mind of the seventies, Walt's words *prepared, deepening burden,* and willingness to *accept cheerfully,* might reflect a strange weakness of character, of not being with it, of capitulating to the establishment, of smashing head-on with the concept of doing your own thing. But Walt was later to prove that his was not a weak character.

His physical appearance, also, might have seemed less than strong with his slim, one-hundred-thirty-pound, five-foot seven-inch frame—but Walt was to prove differently on that score too.

Gil Dodds, eleven-year world record holder for the indoor mile and former track coach at Wheaton College, met Walt in 1950 after Walt went out for football and was turned down. "He came into the gym," said Gil, "and said he wanted to try out for track and cross-country. I looked at this rumpled little guy with his thick owl-like glasses and slow, stumbling speech and wondered how he ever expected me to make anything out of him. When he got into his track gear and tried out, I knew he was the last person I could ever expect to win. He was twenty-six, bowlegged, and didn't have speed.

"But," continued Gil, "I soon began to eat my thoughts. Because I noticed Wally had the qualities of greatness; the kind you can't measure but which all coaches look for. He had great follow-through and was foolish and responsible enough to do everything the coaches told him. But more than that, Wally just plainly had guts and compensated for his lack of natural ability with his attitude, philosophy, and value structure."

Walt knew Coach Dodds believed in him and showed his gratitude the following year by winning the annual

Thanksgiving Turkey Run. Wally's picture and the following article appeared in the *Chicago Tribune:*

> Walter Steinkraus of Wheaton College defeated his
> more illustrious teammate, Cookie Moriya, Loyola
> Invitational and College Conference of Illinois cham-
> pion, to set a record of 15:29:1 in winning yesterday's
> 19th Catholic Youth Organization Turkey Cross-
> Country Run. The former record for the three-mile
> 188 yard Waveland course in Lincoln Park was 15:44,
> set by George Lynch in 1950. Moriya was second,
> almost 26 seconds behind Steinkraus . . . .

Walt followed this by quietly winning the two-mile conference meet during his sophomore, junior, and senior
years.

"I suppose one reason I liked Wally," said Gil, "was
because he reminded me a little of myself. Like Wally,
my coach told me I didn't have form or speed. But like
me, he had stamina and stick-to-itiveness. Wally was the
kind of person who could tolerate fatigue and discomforts
of the flesh. Often during practice I knew Wally was in
pain but he never quit; he kept right on going. When he
had times of discouragement or was disappointed I never
really knew it because he had a lot of rubber and bounced
right back."

Like all good coaches, Gil worked hard on Walt's
strengths to make them stronger. And Walt came through
by qualifying in his senior year for the national collegiate
four-mile meet. In 1955 this was held in East Lansing,
Michigan, and of the best four-milers in the nation, Walter
Steinkraus placed tenth. "Which showed," said Gil, "even

though he didn't look like much of an athlete, he had something deep inside."

This something *deep inside* came partly from a highly developed tenacity which seems to be a natural characteristic among people of Teutonic ancestry—and especially among people who farm the land and fight hard against Michigan winters in Gladwin County.

But the other part came from a distinctly pioneer American life-style. It was a mixture of two-and-a-quarter-mile hikes to Gladwin County's one-room North Sage Elementary School and hide-and-seek in the sweet-smelling hay barn. Sometimes it was a stomach-twinkling ice-skating party on a stiffly frozen lake under a bright, clear December moon—stomach-twinkling because Walt and his younger brother, Sam, usually skated without their doting mother's approval. But mostly it was a practical mixture of clearing land, plowing and harvesting, milking cows, and a once-a-week eight-mile buggy ride to the Round Lake German Baptist Church.

A bird's-eye view of Walt's early life shows it not too dissimilar from that of hundreds of other Michigan farm boys in the early thirties. He was one of ten children and oldest of the three boys. He had a round of farm chores to complete before and after school. He boxed, took part in the drama club, played football in high school, and in spite of his undersized frame was the outstanding defensive tackle of the small Gladwin High School Conference.

But there were differences and they began early in Walt's young life. Each morning and afternoon, Walt pulled his wagon around the farm, which, from a distance, looked like any other young boy pulling a heavy load in a small wagon. But closer examination revealed the load to be his father!

Cruelly crippled with arthritis, Dan Steinkraus valiantly taught his oldest son the rudiments of farming from the cramped deck of his son's play wagon. Mr. Steinkraus knew his son's shoulders were prematurely overloaded with heavy responsibilities. But he also knew fragile Walter was the only link between losing or keeping his farm and family together.

"I was two years younger than Walter," said his brother, Sam. "I still remember helping Walt pull Dad in the wagon when Walt was nine and our brother, Willy, five. Dad was in constant pain but would raise himself up on his thin arms and teach Walt how to milk cows, dig out rocks, build and mend fences."

The other differences were not quite as obvious—unless you shared a breakfast or Sunday afternoon with the Steinkraus family.

"Our mother was a woman of strong character," said Walt's older sister, Edna (now Mrs. Harvey Gertz), "and she insisted we read the Bible and sing hymns after every breakfast. Since she only knew a few words in English, we all read and sang in German. In fact, Walter spoke German before he learned to speak English.

"Today's young people," continued Edna, "would probably find it boring to sit in the living room on a Sunday afternoon and play Bible quiz games. But it wasn't for us. We all looked forward to this as the highlight of our week. In fact, we were happy just to be with each other and enjoy each other's company."

Sam remembers those days as being filled with hard work. But their father's illness, hard work, and pulling hard together, created a great family closeness. This close family sensitivity was demonstrated when at age nine, Sam came forward in an old-fashioned revival meeting and indicated his desire to follow Christ, just as Walt had done two days earlier.

"It was Walt's step of faith that influenced me to believe," said Sam. "Walt was more serious than the rest of us and always meant what he said. I knew Walt wouldn't walk down the church aisle unless it was important. And I thought, if it's important for Walt to take Jesus Christ into his life, I don't want to be left out."

Shortly after Walt's birth, his mother, Malvina, dedicated him to the Lord with a prayer that he would be a preacher. From the beginning it was decided, in spite of heavy farm responsibilities, that Walt should go to high school at all cost. And when Walt publicly confessed his faith in Christ, Malvina praised God that her prayers were on the way to being answered. Then disaster struck and momentarily robbed Malvina and the family of their joy.

It was 1934, the middle of the Great Depression—breadlines, people walking the streets looking for work, bank failures, and for the Steinkraus family, property trouble. Edna, who a year earlier had left home to work in Chicago as a domestic, heard the news first from Walt. In a simple noncomplaining note he wrote:

. . . Our folks lost the farm by not being able to meet the payments. We have moved in with Grandmother Steinkraus . . . .

Four years later, in 1938 after the death of his grandmother, Walt, his father, mother, Willy, Sam, and sisters, Violet, Marge, and Marie, moved for the second time. Money from the grandmother's estate provided the family with another chance to farm the land in Gladwin County. The other sisters, now married, had left home for the big city. Mr. Steinkraus found it increasingly difficult to go outside. Walt now became the man of the family and with his brothers had complete responsibility for running the farm. He was fourteen.

For the following nine years, life in the Steinkraus home settled into a quiet routine of normal farm living. Walt became president of the Round Lake Church young people's group and squeezed this in between school, sports, and heavy farm chores. There were, however, three high moments during that nine-year period.

One was the acquisition of an old secondhand car to drive the family to church. Their move placed them twelve miles from church, and it was becoming increasingly difficult to rely on the kindness of neighbors for transportation.

The second was having Walt's name listed on the honor roll in *Sparks*, the Gladwin High School newspaper. And the third was a graduation suit for Walt. Edna, who regularly sent money home to help the family, dug deeper into her meager savings and bought Walt his first suit, "Because," said Edna, "he was the first in the family to graduate from high school."

After graduation, Malvina expected her young son to fulfill her high expectations by moving into some kind of Bible training. But Walt had other ideas. He chose instead to enroll in a Chicago electrical trade school. Walt's farm experience developed his natural dexterity for detail work, and he felt electrical wiring would add to his vocational skills.

Then halfway through his course, something happened to change Walt's mind. "I don't know how or why it happened," he wrote home, "but I am convinced I should prepare myself to serve the Lord full time. At first I thought this was my own feeling because if it is the Lord's calling, why didn't He show me this before I made plans to come to trade school? Besides, I don't see how I can go to Bible school when I still have responsibilities at home."

As hard as Walt tried to reason away his convictions, the harder the Lord seemed to burden him with the thought of full-time service. Walt had no peace until he told the Lord he would serve full time if He made it possible for him to get proper training. And then he prayed that the Lord would confirm this new sense of direction with specific circumstances.

The circumstances were specific and came sooner than Walt or his family expected. Shortly after Walt wrote home, the Steinkrauses decided the warm, dry climate in Arizona would ease Dan's deteriorating arthritic condition. In a soul-wrenching experience, Walt came home and helped the family put up their house, equipment, and belongings for auction. They traded the land for two small cement-block duplexes and a small one-room unit at the rear of the lot in Phoenix, Arizona.

The change from rural Michigan farm life to urbanized living in Phoenix was surprisingly swift and uncomplicated. The climate change seemed to help Mr. Steinkraus. Walt and the rest of the family immediately joined and

became active in the Phoenix First Missionary Church.
Willy now assumed responsibility for his parents, and in-
come from the duplexes relieved most financial pressures.
This also released Walt to seriously pursue his all-consum-
ing desire to get money to go to school and become properly trained for the Lord's service. This new trend pleased
Walt's mother, who couldn't understand why he had gone
to trade school in the first place after she had dedicated
him to the Lord's service.

Walt's list of jobs between 1947 and 1950 looked like
ingredients from a giant shish kebab. He began in the
South and followed the nation's grapefruit, orange, let-
tuce, tomato, potato, and wheat harvest north. When these
were over, he worked for a Phoenix air-conditioning company. "But," said Willy, "Walt always said it was money
from the wheat harvest that paid his way to Wheaton
College." The wheat harvest and selling his old car may
have started Walt on his way to Wheaton, but it was his
carpentry work with the Copeland Construction Company that got him through his four years.

Walt's fellow students at Wheaton remember him as a
"serious, courageous kind of guy with a dry sense of
humor." He is also remembered by some as a person who
studied hard in the library and never showed much interest in girls. Yet those who attended Wheaton's Ninety-
Fifth Annual Commencement Exercises didn't find Walter
Leinhart Steinkraus among those receiving honor degrees.
His teachers remember him as a beginning *C* student who,
by hard diligent work, pulled himself up to a *B*. "The one
exception," said one teacher, "was a constant *A* in Physical
Education."

While Walt didn't distinguish himself as a dazzling

academician, he graduated with a clear understanding of what he wanted to do and why he had gone to college. The *why* for Wheaton was always before him in the words of Albert Nichols, Wheaton's director of admissions.

. . . We trust your time at Wheaton will be for you not merely an opening to continue your schooling, but in a real sense be an opportunity for the beginning of a sound foundation for the service which you are preparing to give to the Lord and to your fellow citizens in the years to come.

One of the opportunities Walt took advantage of at Wheaton was regularly to attend the Foreign Missions Fellowship meetings. As he learned of the various missionary organizations and their need for personnel, he felt a natural desire to serve the Lord overseas.

While overseas missionary service dominated his thinking during his senior year, Walt didn't forget his home mission opportunities. In a letter to a young fellow he once met and witnessed to, he wrote:

Dear Ken,

Perhaps you don't remember me, yet I hope you do. I wanted to write sooner but kept putting it off. I think often of you, and I often talk to my Lord about you. You remember I talked with you in your home. I wish I could visit with you again, but this will have to be second best.

Life is great. You remember you were going to read the Gospel of John. I wish I could talk to you about it. What could I wish more but that you have already found the true life. What makes it sad is that so many do not know this great life. In John 20:31 it says: "But these are written, that ye might believe that Jesus is the Christ, the Son of God; and that believing ye might have life through his name." Since Jesus is the Son of God, then if He says we have life by believing in Him, we can be sure of it. In other words, we can put our trust in Him, since He died in our place. Ken, if you do not know Jesus yet, why don't you say YES to Him right now. It will be the best and most important thing you ever did. God's Word says: "But as many as received him, to them gave he power to become the sons of God, even to them that believe on his name" (John 1:12).

God loved us so much that He gave His all to save us, so when we don't accept Him it's the most tragic thing we can do. It's like turning our back and slamming the door in the face of the Holy God and saying I'll go my own way. It's worse than tragic; see John 3:18.

How are you? Write me a card saying how you are coming along. I like it here.

Your friend,

*Walter Steinkraus*

After graduation in 1954, Walt further prepared himself by spending a fall semester at Fort Wayne Bible College in Indiana. Here, during a phonetics course, Walt saw the future direction of his life fall into place. The missions fellowship groups at Wheaton guided him to see the need for world missions, and now through the study of sounds, Walt saw the vehicle he would use to meet that need. He was challenged by Wycliffe Bible Translators and their practical use of descriptive linguistics and cultural anthropology. He saw Wycliffe to be a unique and exciting linguistic organization that was reaching out to the world's ethnic minorities with the good news of God's love through Bible translation.

Yet, however grand Walt's ideals were, he needed money to make them come true, because joining Wycliffe as a Bible translator meant the prerequisite of an eleven-week linguistic training course at one of the Summer Institutes of Linguistics (S.I.L.). Walt chose the courses offered at the University of Oklahoma at Norman—but only after he spent the spring driving nails, sawing two-by-fours, and framing up houses for the Copeland Construction Company.

S.I.L.'s intensive nature causes most first-year students to find the beginning two weeks of linguistic training mentally analogous to the intensive physical pain and exhaustion that occurs during the first two weeks of fall football training. Walt, like most others, stumbled and grappled with craggy-edged concepts found in new words like morphology, linear phonemes, avilar fricatives, syntax, segmentation, contextual variants, and nonaspiration.

The patient Wycliffe teaching staff at S.I.L. encouraged the students to "hang in," remembering their own mental stumblings. They knew the fog would lift sometime during the first two or three weeks. Walt, like hundreds before and since, suddenly saw the intensive courses in morphology, phonetics, and phonemics as more than a madman's contrivance to test one's wits! He began to understand that the courses were equipping him with highly specialized tools and methodology to probe deep into the phenomenally complex study of human culture and language.

There was, however, one complex study of human behavior that Walt discovered without the aid of the experienced S.I.L. staff. It's called "falling in love." He saw her first on the tennis court—a bright, fresh, vivaciously happy brown-haired second-year student and Wycliffe member, LaVonne Schreurs. She was playing tennis with a fellow named Harry, and for the first time in his life Walt found himself wishing he had gained proficiency in tennis, rather than cross-country.

# 2 *That Ol' Banker!*

Walt didn't know it then, but if he had asked this cute little bundle of energy thwacking sizzling nonreturnable serves to run with him, she probably would have accepted. Because LaVonne (Vonnie) Jean Schreurs lived for sports and all outdoor activity.

So varied were her hobbies and sports activities that when Vonnie filled out her official seven-page Wycliffe application form in 1954, she ran out of space for the question, "What sports do you engage in?" With her thick-nibbed fountain pen she wrote: Hiking, skating, horseback riding, skiing, golf, volleyball, basketball, Ping-Pong, swimming, and tennis. For the question, "What sports do you show a degree of proficiency in?" she wrote: Swimming, horseback riding, tennis, golf, skating. For her occupational skills she listed: Nursing, gardening, sewing, cooking, plant culture, tropical fish, singing, photography. Which is, if you ask anyone from the Badger State, about average for natives from Sheboygan, Wisconsin.

The 294 Tri-State Tollway running north from Chicago will take you to Sheboygan should you want to go. It first dissects the industrial city of Milwaukee, then skims along the Lake Michigan coastline through Sheboygan on its way to Green Bay and the Michigan border. The land is rich, rolling, and clustered with blue silos, orange red barns, and brown and white jigsaw-patterned guernsey dairy cattle.

The land is also rich with a surprising amount of notable firsts. Wisconsin is the birthplace of the Republican Party and the nation's first kindergarten. Ringling Brothers created the first big top at Baraboo. The first practical typewriter came from Milwaukee, and its Swiss, Danish, and Norwegian immigrants gave the state its distinction as the nation's dairyland.

Wisconsin is a healthy, active state where the spirit of *Gemütlichkeit* (good fellowship) spills out from the buoyancy of its many ethnic festivals. A visitor in May might be caught up in the middle of hardy red-cheeked Norwegians celebrating their national day of independence. A later visitor might catch energetic teen-agers of Polish parentage training hard for their mountaineer dance. Or catch the German Bratwurst Festival in Milwaukee or the Swiss William Tell Pageant in New Glarus.

And if you happen to drive down elm-lined South Fifteenth Street in Sheboygan and stop beside a two-story white frame house at 1311, you might, with the right kind of eyes and ears and turning time back to 1940, catch the true spirit of *Gemütlichkeit*. It's the happy home of Nora and Arthur Schreurs—a home sparkling with the freedom of mutual love, trust, and respect which spilled over into the lives of their two daughters, Vonnie and her fifteen-month older sister, Phyllis (Phyll).

The early forties had its own problems, but raising chil-

dren didn't seem to be one of them. At least not for the
Schreurs family living in Sheboygan.

"I let the girls do pretty much what they wanted to do,"
said Mrs. Schreurs, "and never had any trouble."

Vonnie and Phyll were great buddies and spent every
moment they could out-of-doors. In the summer they
swam in the old quarry and ran barefoot across the sand
dunes by the lake.

"We both thought this was the best way to make our
legs strong," recalls Phyll. "And at thirteen and fifteen
we thought nothing was more important than having
strong legs!"

For Vonnie and Phyll strong legs were indeed important. How else could they scamper and run over their
widowed grandfather's sixty-acre dairy farm at Cedar
Grove, fourteen miles south of Sheboygan?

The weekly visits to the farm were magical. The farm-
house was big and white, the barn was red and there was
a blacksmith's shop filled with old horseshoes. And adding
to the magic was a jack-of-all-trades Dutch grandfather
with thick white hair and bushy eyebrows. "I liked him
very much," said Phyll, "but was a little afraid of him. He
could be stern and I think he liked Vonnie better than me
because I talked too much."

Judging by their ceaseless activity on the farm, it's hard
to believe Vonnie or Phyll took time to talk to anyone. In
the hot, sticky summers they would grab a bar of Ivory
soap and race down to Lake Michigan (their grandfather's
land ran right up to the shore) and wash themselves clean
with a cool refreshing bath. At night the girls drifted off
into a delicious sleep to the sound of chirping crickets and
the sweet smell of their straw-filled mattresses.

In the fall they ran up and down the leaf-filled gullies and took long walks in the woods. And in spring when the ice melted, the two sisters dammed the little runoff creeks and made big pools of clear, cold water.

When they didn't go to the farm, they spent their spare time at the Riverdale Riding Stable, where they helped clean out the barn and curry the horses for a free ride (fifty cents an hour was more than they could afford).

"We'd ride through the woods," said Phyll, "and end up cantering them through the willows and back across the sand dunes. It was a wonderful time to be alive!"

Both Vonnie and Phyll loved sports but it was Vonnie who captured their zest for life. In 1940 at age twelve, she began a lifelong habit of recording daily events of her active life. Her prose then, and later as an adult, was pithy, refreshing, and reflected her love affair with life and unusual sensitivity to the magic of the mundane. Vonnie saw the beauty of reflected light through a jar of preserves, or the buzz of a housefly on a quiet spring morning on the farm.

Her 1940 diary began:

January 2—Had teeth fixed. Went to Aunty Eliza's and played with Skippy the dog. Then went shopping with Mom and Phyllis.

January 5—Went to school. Had gym, played Steal the Bacon. Our side won 16 to 10. I made the first score.

January 6—Went to swimming class, school. Came home and went ice skating. Came home, ate supper, and went back skating.

January 12—Had bad cold. Daddy didn't want me to go to school, but I did. Had chinning test. I only got up eight times.

January 14—Went to Sunday school. Got a book for perfect attendance. Shovelled walk in P.M. Listened to Edgar Bergen and Charlie McCarthy.

January 15—Played Parcheesi at Seven O'Clock Club. I won. Daddy brought us all some ice cream.

January 24—Quite a snow storm. After supper went sledding with Phyllis and Harold. He got mad and broke his bobsled which he made.

February 11—Went for long walk with Daddy. We played in our ice cave.

February 14—I got seventeen valentines.

Vonnie's winter world was sledding, music lessons, swimming (indoors), Sunday school and Thursday Bible class at the Christian Reformed Church, skating, and Girl Scouts. Then came her March entry:

March 25—Chopped ice so water could run down the sewer. Had lots of fun.

Her spring baseball activity was interrupted with this important entry:

May 8—Got a bicycle. And am I glad it's blue and white. I don't know how to ride yet.

May 9—Got up early. Barbara helped me learn to ride. Fell down a couple of times on Lake Shore Drive.

May 10—Am riding my bicycle pretty good now.

The year 1940 was an important vacation year for Vonnie and her family. Her diary tells of a June trip to Washington, D.C., the New York World's Fair, Niagara Falls, and Dearborn, Michigan. Her two important observations were that the Washington Monument had 898 steps and the Statue of Liberty had 365.

In July, Vonnie's world became summer school, bike riding, and strawberry picking. She noted, "Made $1.53 in two days."

From July to December there are only a few scattered references to her activities. But she ended the year with this:

> December 29—I got a prize for perfect attendance at church and Sunday school four years straight.

Vonnie's 1941 diary shows her continued interest in sports which now included horseback riding, basketball, volleyball, and important hikes to Horseshoe Bend, "where we get real pussy willows."

"Vonnie so loved flowers and plants," said her mother, "that she used to scrounge in the neighbors' garbage cans for flowers they might have thrown away."

The first hint that Vonnie's behavior was not all it should be came in her March 4 and 5 entries.

> March 4—Went to catechism. Me and Fay got marked down for behavior. We were laughing too much.
> March 5—Me and Lillian went singing in the halls at school and got into trouble.

And like most fourteen year olds, Vonnie occasionally chafed under parental authority.

> June 5—Went to school. Mother cleaning house. I HAD to cut the lawn.

> June 13—I have mumps. I had to stay in bed all day.
>     I listened to radio.
> June 14—I was supposed to stay in bed but I didn't.
>     I wish I could go outside.

On June 17 she did. And on the twenty-fifth, Vonnie
and her father went fishing. "Caught one fish. After supper
went fishing again. I caught two fish."

From July 25 to August 10, the Schreurs family took
their yearly vacation. Vonnie's record shows: "We started
trip at Twin Cities, then drove through the Black Hills
and Badlands of South Dakota. Saw the Presidents' faces
at Mt. Rushmore. They were big and beautiful. Saw Cus-
ter's battlefields. Drove to Yellowstone Park and saw Old
Faithful erupt four times. Saw 17 bears, 3 deer, 1 moose,
and 1 wolf. Went swimming in Salt Lake. You float like
a cork. Went to Pike's Peak which is 14,110 feet high.
Came home after seeing Cave of the Wind. Had two flats."

In 1943 Vonnie turned fifteen. Her diary showed continued interest in sports with the addition of bowling and
the shot put which she threw twenty-one feet. It also
showed her development into womanhood.

> January 4—We had a movie at school and I saw
>     "Boing." Gee, he's cute—Boing! Oh, well, I can
>     dream.

On January 25 after a month of bowling, basketball,
swimming, being made basketball captain, and "almost
getting kicked out of music," she notes, "Almost broke my
neck in a skiing accident." Her diary then continues:

January 30—Went to school. Gave report in English
and made a big mess of things. Had to go to my
seat twice before I could finish.

February 5—Saw ———. He didn't even look at me
when I said hi—only at Phyllis.

February 6—Had movie at school. Was it good! Especially the swell horses.

It seemed only a matter of time before Vonnie would
have to "come to grips with her schoolwork," as her teachers would say. Vonnie knew she was not doing the best
she could. Her teachers told her this from kindergarten.
Nevertheless she sandwiched her schoolwork between
choir practice, a multiplicity of sports, and having fun.

February 7—Got report card. *F* in English, *F* in Geom-
etry, *G* in Latin, *G*+ in choir and *E* in Gym. Felt
good today. Had fun.

March 20—Went to school. Lillian, Stella, Dolly and
me got kicked out of library for two weeks for
laughing.

It was also in March that Vonnie began working at the
Lakeland Manufacturing Company on Saturdays. Her
March 30 entry records, "Had to work all day. Got hol-
lered at by big boss. After supper went horseback riding.
Ruth's horse threw her so I chased after it until I lost him."

Vonnie's April 5 entry showed an early character trait
that became a trademark to those who knew and worked
with her. For some it was exasperating; for those who
knew her best, it endeared her to them. Said one friend
years later, "When I heard Vonnie wanted to go to the
jungles of Peru, I wondered who was going to save her

from herself. She always seemed to be in another world
and nothing shook her."

> April 5—After school went to lifesaving. Swam 35
> lengths of pool. On way home missed first bus,
> missed second, third bus was the wrong bus. Got
> a transfer, then missed another bus. Gee, I was all
> mixed up.

There was, however, one person who managed to shake
Vonnie—Miss Banker.

> May 4—B. Garling and I got our seats changed. Miss
> Banker put me right in front of her so she could
> keep an eye on me. But Stella and I were writing
> notes all period.

The June graduation exercises held at Volrath Park were
always as exciting for the undergraduates as the graduates
—except Vonnie, that year.

> June 13—Went to school. Got report card. Got two *Es*,
> two *Gs*, and two *Fs*. That ol' Banker gave me an
> *F* again. Boy is she bad. And to think I get her
> next year. Phooey! Went to bed.

June of 1943 was a difficult month for Vonnie. She went
to summer camp and fell head-over-heels for Jim. But Jim
was already committed.

> June 26—At night we went to camp and went walking
> with the boys. I walked with Bud but I don't
> like him. Jim was with Dot again. Phooey.

July 6—Went swimming at the quarry. Saw Jim again. He was with his girl friend but was nice to me. Anyway his girl friend is a good swimmer, too.

Vonnie had three notable entries in August, October, and November.

August 14—Went to work. Took the radio along to hear the war bulletin. Peace was proclaimed so I took the car and called the kids and went running around. Was Dad mad! Then went uptown with the gang. It sure was crowded. Everyone was having a swell time. Got home about 2:00. Never have I seen so many cars and people and good humor.

October 31—After school went to work. After supper went Halloweening with the kids. We had lots of fun throwing rotten tomatoes, breaking bottles, letting air out of tires, carrying away benches and waxing windows. Only one cop chased us.

November 14—Got report card. I got two *Es*, three *Gs*, and one *F* from that ol' Banker.

# 3 "Cut!"

"I guess it all started when an elder in the Brethren Assembly asked me if I was saved," said Phyllis. "I was coming out of the Sunday night service and all of a sudden I was faced with this question. I was stunned for a moment and looked at him. Then because my strong Dutch Reform background strictly taught me to always tell the truth, I answered with a truthful *no*."

The elder then asked Phyllis if she wouldn't like to be saved. She answered with a weak, "I suppose so," and that night, through the words of Isaiah 53, Phyllis saw that Jesus not only loved her but suffered and died like a criminal in her place on the cross.

"Our home," said Phyllis, "was always a happy place and Mom and Dad were careful to teach Vonnie and me the right way to live, based on what they believed to be Christian teaching. But that night the matter of being saved or allowing Jesus to control my thinking and personality all became very personal and I suddenly understood that I had to make a choice. And I did!"

Phyllis not only chose to follow the Lord that Sunday night, she chose to begin a life-style that completely baffled Vonnie. In her youthful enthusiasm to introduce

friends to her new Friend and faith, Phyllis conspicu-
ously carried her Bible to school, and gave up interests
and activities that weren't church-related.

"Vonnie used to laugh and call me a fundamentalist
fanatic," said Phyllis, "and while this upset me, I never
got mad at her. Vonnie's laugh seemed to come right
from the tips of her toes and was so contagious, I always
ended up laughing with her."

Vonnie's good-natured laughter and unusual activity
were seen by most as enviable attributes—except by her
pastor, the Reverend Ellis Mooney, a jaunty, energetic
man who loved the Schreurs family but felt Vonnie was
using this to mask her unresolved spiritual responsibilities.
"After she graduated from Central High School and en-
rolled in Rockford College in Rockford, Illinois," said
Reverend Mooney, "I just felt Vonnie was running away
from the Lord."

Most people over thirty probably remember the events
of 1947. Car enthusiasts will remember this was the year
Henry Kaiser introduced his now-defunct Kaiser auto-
mobile. And those interested in hair styles will remember
magazines asking, "Which twin has the Toni?" But 1947
still burns brightly in Phyllis's mind as the year Vonnie
stopped running from the Lord.

"It was early in September," said Phyllis. "Virginia Fel-
ton, a mutual friend, and I bought a big bag of green
grapes and munched on them all the way over to visit
Vonnie in Rockford. I was still young in my faith and
took Virginia along to help me explain to Vonnie how
and why she should let Christ control her life."

In years to come, Phyllis and Virginia would cherish
this moment in time, believing that after pleading with

Vonnie to accept Christ, she did. But what they didn't know was that Vonnie's *yes* had reservations. She had trouble believing evangelical Christians were not fanatical kooks. It wasn't until she accepted an invitation to Wheaton College's Homecoming several weeks later that Phyllis's and Virginia's words fell into place.

Vonnie wrote in her diary that she accepted the invitation only to prove to herself once and for all that evangelical Christianity was nothing more than religious fanaticism. Vonnie did prove something to herself that weekend. But it wasn't that her sister and Virginia were religious fanatics. "I proved," said Vonnie, "that I wasn't all I thought I was spiritually. I knew from our teaching at home, Sunday school, and church that God wanted us to live a moral, upright life. But after that weekend, it suddenly dawned on me that I had to make a decision to either accept and live my life the way God wanted, or reject this and live the way I wanted."

Vonnie returned to Rockford and immediately began a serious, thoughtful study of her Bible. Carefully she looked up recommended passages of Scripture from a gospel tract Phyllis had given her. Then in her diary, Vonnie wrote these amazing words:

> October 19, 1947—Oh, happy day when Jesus came into my heart to stay, 2 Corinthians 5:17. After carefully reading and rereading my Bible and selected verses, it seemed that God was speaking just to me. And this afternoon I have accepted Jesus Christ into my life as my Saviour.

Immediately following this paragraph, Vonnie wrote: "This very evening God impressed me about preparing myself for full-time Christian service on the mission field."

Several weeks later she told Phyllis that she wasn't going to state a preference for a field of service. "I'll trust Him to send me where He wants me to go," she said.

Vonnie's preparation and leading began first with a summer at the University of Wisconsin after her year at Rockford College. She followed this in the fall of 1948 by enrolling for nurses' training at Chicago's West Suburban Hospital in Oak Park.

West Suburban's affiliation with Wheaton College and its honored reputation for professional excellence attracts dedicated Christian students from a wide geographical spectrum. Vonnie's beginning class drew nursing enthusiasts from Brazil, the Ivory Coast, Canada, South Africa, California, New York, Florida, and a girl friend from Sheboygan. Like Vonnie, most chose nursing as a positive way to express their Christian concern and responsibility to help others.

Vonnie earned her R.N. degree at West Suburban and a B.S. degree from Wheaton after four years of hard work, sleepless nights, and becoming a legend among her contemporaries. She wasn't, in the words of one of her supervisors, an A student, but she was a good nurse because she had people at heart and wanted to reach out and touch them physically and spiritually.

One of Vonnie's friends who shared an apartment with her recalls Vonnie's extraordinary capacity to always be going somewhere or doing something. If Moody Founder's Week happened to conflict with her studies, she went to Founder's Week. And if a party came up the night before an exam, she took in the party. "Vonnie was the kind who seemed to get by on almost no sleep," said her friend.

While it was true that Vonnie was an all-around girl who needed to be continually active, her activity included a growing interest in Christian service and outreach. She regularly helped in the canteen and with the witnessing staff at the Pacific Garden Mission in downtown Chicago. And if no one wanted to go with her, she went alone.

"We all liked Vonnie," said Winnie Christensen, author of "Caught with My Mouth Open" and former classmate of Vonnie's. "We loved her because she was a truly delightful person to have around and because she was responsible for some of the funniest things that happened to us in class."

All of her classmates remember with great hilarity the time she was scrubbed for a cystostomy (bladder operation) and assisted Dr. M., a notorious grouch with a violent temper who demanded immediate action whenever he barked an order. Part of the equipment that Vonnie was responsible for during the operation was a large irrigator that stood on a stand above her head. Its function was to flush away blood and clean the incision with a saline water solution. The plastic tube leading from the irrigator through the incision to the disposal unit had a simple clamp device that cut the flow whenever the doctor wanted it stopped.

On this day, true to his reputation, Dr. M. vociferated a sharp, "Cut!" In her eagerness to act promptly, Vonnie reached into her pocket and with her ever-ready bandage scissors, severed the tube! When Dr. M. saw the water spurting out across his sterile field, he couldn't believe what his eyes told him. For the first time in his life he was beyond temper. Later when he asked for the name of the assisting nurse, Vonnie's friends demonstrated their true affection by refusing to divulge her name.

Vonnie's classic ability for never getting shook up or losing her cool evidenced itself on another occasion when she was working in the diet kitchen where an absolutely unbreakable rule said, "No eating." But hunger got the better of Vonnie and she picked up a leftover piece of food from a tray. As destiny would have it, her supervisor walked into the room at that precise moment and with an icy voice said, "MISS SCHREURS! What are you doing?" Without a moment's hesitation and in perfect calmness, Vonnie turned around, looked at her, smiled, and said innocently, "I'm eating."

Throughout her nurses' training at West Suburban and later studies at Wheaton, Vonnie's friends continued to see her as a carefree, often dreamy person, not too interested in fashion or heavy dating. They also remember her as a girl who couldn't judge distance and believed her when she said her father joked about her repeatedly knocking the bumper off the family car as she tried to back it into the garage.

They further knew no one contacted motion sickness faster or harder than Vonnie. So when Vonnie announced her intention, after seeing the Wycliffe film, *O For a Thousand Tongues,* to spend a summer at the Summer Institute of Linguistics with the hope of joining Wycliffe Bible Translators, they laughed. Not to be cruel but because Vonnie seemed such an unlikely candidate for the mission field.

When Vonnie's friends laughed and kidded her, she laughed with them. She was comfortable in her growing faith and felt the supportive love of her many friends.

"Yet because she had so many friends," said a friend, "I don't believe anyone got real close."

If they could have, they would have seen a deeply sensitive, contemplative person with a capacity for decisive action when it was truly required.

Not many people ever found out about it, but Vonnie's ability not to get flustered once saved fifteen-year-old Phyllis from a watery grave in Lake Michigan. After an afternoon of sledding on their grandfather's farm one cheerless day in mid-January, Phyllis, Vonnie, and their cousin decided to have a closer look at the ice that was building up along Lake Michigan's shoreline. The girls pulled up their coat collars and walked toward the deserted beach while hard-driving winds splashed ink green water onto an ice flow etched by wind and water to form slippery steps leading down to the water's edge. As Phyllis started down, she suddenly slipped on the wet surface of the sloping ice. The more she scrambled to walk or crawl, the more she slipped and slid closer to the water's edge. Phyllis knew a fall into the water would be the end. With her heavy clothes, boots, and the numbing cold, there would be no way out.

Quickly, Vonnie, in her characteristic nothing-ever-bothers-me attitude, pushed out the sled and hung onto the long pull rope. With a great sigh of relief, Phyllis grabbed the runners and Vonnie and her cousin pulled her back to safety.

If Vonnie's friends wondered about her unflusterability, her father didn't. He viewed it as unmitigated optimism. After her graduation from Wheaton College in 1952, Vonnie cheerily announced her intention to spend a summer at Wycliffe's Summer Institute of Linguistics in Norman, Oklahoma, and after that, in the fall to go to Columbia Bible College in South Carolina.

"And where," said her father with a half-smile, "do you expect to get the money for all this?"

"I'll just get a job," said Vonnie confidently.

"And I suppose you plan to get a job," answered her father, snapping his fingers, "just like that."

Vonnie chuckled, smiled, and exposed her big dimples. "Yes," she said.

"And," said her father, "Vonnie went out that morning and got a job at Sheboygan Memorial Hospital."

Nine months later, in July of 1953, Vonnie began a hot, exciting, frustrating, mind-expanding eleven weeks of linguistic training at the Summer Institute of Linguistics at the University of Oklahoma in Norman. The following July, in 1954, she returned for an intermediate course of linguistic study. In between, from September, 1953, to June, 1954, she studied hard at Columbia Bible College's Graduate School of Mission in South Carolina.

Columbia could have been Vonnie's silent, least colorful school experience. Her diary-keeping was almost non-existent. If it hadn't been for her letters home, few would have known how important this year was. Columbia taught her, as no other experience before, the importance of a regular quiet time of Scripture reading, prayer, and meditation—a habit she tried to maintain for the rest of her adult life. With greater attention to what God was teaching her through His Word, Vonnie began to grapple with one of Christianity's basic and perhaps most difficult concepts—complete submission to God's wishes. She began a conscious effort to govern her choices and actions with the preface, "Teach me to do Thy will, for Thou art my God." And because she knew and experienced God's love, Vonnie responded in reciprocal love by obeying the impulses of God's leading. When she returned for the intermediate linguistics course in the summer of 1954, she explained it all in a formal letter of application to the candidate office of the Summer Institute of Linguistics and Wycliffe Bible Translators.

> . . . During this past year while a student at Columbia Bible College, God continued to speak to me concerning taking further training in linguistics. I returned this summer knowing it was His will for me to be here. The Lord has increased my love for His Word and given me a burden for the unreached tribes of the world. After seeing a Wycliffe film during nurses' training, it has been my desire, if the Lord continues to lead, to help translate His Word for a tribe that has never heard of the Lord Jesus Christ.

Like all potential Wycliffe members, Vonnie submitted names of friends, teachers, pastors, and former employers for character references. Her pastor, Reverend Mooney, received a questionnaire and to the question which asked for family background and home conditions, wrote: "Both father and mother are devout and active Christians. Her father is a Gideon, a Christian Businessmen's Committee member, and an excellent teacher and student of the Scriptures."

To the question, "Do you know of any doctrinal point which is not well-balanced," his answer was, "LaVonne is well-balanced and has healthy spiritual attitudes."

Another questionnaire was sent to Columbia Bible College and read:

Dear Friend,
   LaVonne Schreurs has applied for membership in our organization and has given your name as a business reference . . . .

The form then provided appropriate squares to check the financial habits and integrity of said person.

The then assistant treasurer for the college answered the questionnaire but didn't check any of the squares. Instead she wrote across the top, "She was a student here 1953-54 and is due $40.00 balance on her room and board a/c." Then at the bottom of the form marked off in red, the treasurer wrote, "Have just discovered I have mixed LaVonne Schreurs with another student. LaVonne does not owe us anything and was very prompt in meeting her payments!"

In addition, Wycliffe teachers and staff at the Summer Institute of Linguistics filled out their own character evaluations. A summary of their evaluations revealed, "She isn't tops in linguistics but is a good nurse and a good mixer." Another S.I.L. staffer reported her difficulty with sounds and wondered about her C grades in Phonetics. The report went on to say, "Perhaps she would be happier with another organization."

But a staff member who had closely observed Vonnie dispelled any doubts about her ability to grow, develop, tackle, and complete her assigned responsibilities.

"It's true," wrote the staffer, "Vonnie's last year grades and beginning grades this summer were considered poor.

But she has made remarkable progress and shown great drive and determination. And regardless of her personal dislike or seeming lack of qualifications, she has consistently chosen to go ahead with what she believes to be the Lord's leading and looks forward to His next step for her life.

"I became better acquainted with Vonnie during a weekend retreat and was tremendously impressed by her testimony given very sweetly and humbly to a ladies' class. It was through this weekend that I came to know her background. I found out her dislike of Latin and all subjects which involve memorizing mass detail. This is one reason she felt called to be a nurse. She felt the most effective form of evangelism was touching people at a point of need, not just imparting information. But even her nurses' training gave her problems and she had to struggle with her chosen specialty of obstetrics. Then came linguistics and more struggles. But her progress shows how God has met her in these struggles. Her attitude has been a great challenge to me. And I cannot help but notice a parallel between Vonnie's surrender and push in something she finds difficult and dislikes, and the way some of Wycliffe's best scholars and researchers have pushed through on difficult linguistic projects.

"I have heard comments from other intermediate students about Vonnie. All are good. She is, in fact, a very sweet girl and a blessing to be around. I highly recommend her for service with Wycliffe Bible Translators."

Because Vonnie applied late in the summer, many of her references were not available when the Board met at the end of S.I.L.'s term. It wasn't until November 29, 1954, that Vonnie breathlessly tore open an official Wycliffe envelope and read:

Dear Miss Schreurs:

It is a pleasure to inform you that by action of our Board of Directors at a meeting November 27, you were accepted as a junior member of both the Wycliffe Bible Translators, Inc., and the Summer Institute of Linguistics.

May we take this opportunity to welcome you into our Wycliffe family, with the assurance that we, by prayer and devotion to the task committed to us, may ever be "steadfast, always abounding in the work of the Lord."

Sincerely in Christ our Lord,

WYCLIFFE BIBLE TRANSLATORS, INC.
(Signed) *Ken Watters*
Secretary-Treasurer

There was a full rich feeling of stomach-fluttering happiness in Vonnie's voice as she excitedly shared the news with her family. She read the letter a second time. It was true! She was now a Wycliffe member and in less than a month would be on her way to Wycliffe's jungle training camp in southern Mexico, and she was happy, happy, happy!

# 4  *You Learn by Doing*

Her odyssey began early New Year's Day, a Saturday in 1955, after twenty sleepless hours of last-minute packing, a New Year's Eve church service and tear-stained fare-wells. At 3:45 A.M., an efficient Diesel engine pulled Vonnie and her six girl traveling companions away from the antique Sheboygan train station into the blue cold Wisconsin darkness.

The journey to Laredo, Texas, Mexico City, and finally Jungle Camp was tailor-made for Vonnie's love of excitement and high adventure. And although she spent twelve hours of the thirty-seven-hour trip to Laredo without a seat, plus four hours of queasy motion sickness, Vonnie was having a ball. She met new people and enjoyed explaining to wide-eyed passengers she was on her way to live in the jungles of old Mexico. She played games with her friends and talked as only girls can when they're excited about a new experience.

At 4:30 P.M. on Sunday, the train chugged into the bustling Laredo train station. Tired but still excited, all seven checked into the Bendor Hotel and shared an apartment.

The sand-colored two-story Bendor looks more like a

prop from a William Faulkner novel than a community hotel. It comes with a common kitchen, a museum-piece typewriter with dirty keys, and a sagging screen door that clacks and bangs when opened or closed. There's a three-bladed overhead fan in the lobby, a front porch equipped with creaky old men with silver sandpaper beards in rockers, and rooms that start at $3.50 per night.

If any of this bothered Vonnie and her friends they never admitted it. Her diary simply said:

> January 3—Spent day in Laredo. Went shopping, cooked our own meals, had a grand time.
>
> January 4—Met Glory and Betty and they with Jan, Becky, Ruth, Irma, Marie, Priscilla, and me went through Mexican customs and inspection. Then boarded train to Mexico City. For 14 pesos ($1.22) Priscilla and I got a seat on train. Had little sleep during night but had a good day. Meals were good. Visited and met people. Played Rook with a Mexican doctor and his wife we met.

In 1955, headquarters for Wycliffe's Mexico operation was located a dozen blocks from where Vonnie and her friends disembarked. Her only comment about the "Kettle," as Wycliffe Mexico members affectionately nick-named it, was that it was a "good place to be."

Her friends, however, bantered about how cramped and overcrowded the three-story cement building was. Vonnie smiled, but not at their jokes. She saw more than a grimy building sitting in the middle of a concrete jungle sprinkled with falling soot and flaking plaster. The old former hotel with the strange Aztec name of Quetzalcoatl was, for Vonnie, the place where dreams come true. It was here she experienced what she did best—meeting new friends and becoming reacquainted with old friends from S.I.L. But more than that, the "Kettle" symbolized the rich warmth of fellowship and community generated by people voluntarily yielded to God and His service.

"Most Wycliffe workers come from secure, comfortable mechanized homes. And because of this, beginning Wycliffe workers have an immediate problem." The speaker was Earl Adams, the crew-cut, boyish-looking director of Wycliffe's Jungle Camp training program in southern Mexico. Vonnie, along with thirty-five other campers, was busy taking notes during her first day of orientation after arrival at Jungle Camp.

"All of you," continued Earl, "have joined or want to join Wycliffe because you have a desire to share God and His translated Word with people who don't know that God's plan for them and the world is His Son, Jesus Christ. However, before you arrive in your assigned field of service and begin an effective long-range ministry, you must understand something about ethnic peoples and their local conditions and customs. Most of you will share the gospel with people whose life-style is exceedingly different from what you have been used to. This twelve-week Jungle Camp and field training course will ease you as a group and individually into actual field conditions. Before coming to Mexico, most of you heard or read about different ethnic life-styles. However, it's another matter to visit with them in their smoke-filled huts and eat what they eat. It's one thing to read about physical needs of people you want to serve; it's another to be invited to help sew up the results of a drunken machete fight."

Earl Adams continued to lecture and explain that Jungle Camp was a bridge between the known and unknown, expected and unexpected. When Vonnie heard the word *unexpected,* she nodded her head in agreement and momentarily reflected on her past forty-eight hours.

In Mexico City she had looked at a map in the "Kettle" and had seen the tiny Missionary Aviation Base of Ixtapa in the state of Chiapas. This was where she would take the Missionary Aviation plane to Jungle Camp. In round figures she estimated the distance to be about seven hundred miles. "A nice pleasant bus trip," she thought. But the unexpected happened as it would many times during her missionary career. After boarding the bus that would take them toward Jungle Camp, Vonnie and her girl friends discovered a few miles out of Mexico City that the trip would take them through some of the sharpest mountain curves in all Mexico. True to form, the repeated lurching sent Vonnie's stomach into shivering nausea. Instinctively she popped an antimotion-sickness pill into her mouth and waited for it to do its work. It did. But not with the pleasant calming effects she had previously experienced. The pill seemed to speed up her metabolism without helping her motion sickness. After the reaction finally worked itself out, Vonnie faced yet another unexpected detail—the frigid cold of Mexico's high mountain passes in an unheated bus. When the bus ended her ordeal twenty-four hours later in the hot tropical town of Tuxtla Gutierrez, Vonnie and her friends still had a taxi ride that began at 1,800 feet and climbed to almost 4,000 feet in thirty-five miles!

"The Jungle Camp program is designed for each person to learn by doing." Vonnie smiled and agreed with Earl

Adams. She had learned more by doing in the last forty-eight hours than she ever dreamed possible!

There were further lectures that outlined what campers could expect during their training. "For the next six weeks at Main Base, the emphasis will be on team work," said Earl. "This will include a variety of practical everyday skills—cooking (over an open fire), carpentry (using native materials), mechanics (repair of gas pump motors, light plants, gas lanterns), tropical hygiene, swimming, canoeing, trail travel, and camping. After six weeks of conditioning at Main Base, you will all hike about twenty miles to a remote Advance Base site. This is a family-oriented or single-partnership situation where you will put into practice the skills you learn at Main Base."

From other Wycliffites who had taken the course, Vonnie knew Advance Base would be great fun. The idea of gathering her own fuel and building her own shelter and furniture from local materials would not be too different from her earlier farm experience. She was also excited about participating in simulated emergency survival techniques.

"You will take part in all this," said Earl, "after you have had instruction in map reading, raft building, weather forecasting, et cetera. But," emphasized Earl, "there are three important skills we look for above all others. These are an attitude toward team work, self-reliance, and practical relaxed spiritual living. At times you may wonder why we spend time and energy to have you go through this specialized training. If you do, remember our jungle training program is an important factor in maintaining Wycliffe's relatively low dropout rate."

After attending lectures, practical demonstrations, and

getting settled in her nine-by-nine-foot mud-wall grass-roofed hut, Vonnie recorded her day-by-day Jungle Camp experiences.

> January 7—My first impressions of J.C.—lovely!
> January 8—Living with Marie and Becky. Took swim in river (most people think it has its origins in the North Pole!) and went on short hike. Picked over beans and wheat.
> January 11—Class in orientation, Tzeltal language study, carpentry, swimming, and clinic. Went on short hike along a jungle path. Also started with swimming tests.

Vonnie's excellent swimming ability and training in life-saving were immediately put to use when she was asked to teach the advanced women's swimming class. There was only one short line in her diary to indicate this.

> January 12—Butchered cow today. Started teaching advanced swimming.
> January 13—Up at 4:15 to help cook breakfast.
> January 14—Left at 4:00 P.M. for overnight. Jungle hammock can be quite comfortable. I had mine near falls in river.

Vonnie's entries for the next few days listed a more intense round of Jungle Camp activity which included working in the kitchen, visiting Indian villages, devotions, swimming, and killing, defeathering, cutting, and cleaning a chicken. And in the middle of her practical activities she wrote, "Noticed bamboo, orchids, and mistletoe on hike. When I washed clothes and bathed in river, saw and heard the pleasant sounds of chattering monkeys and emerald green parrots in the woods."

On January 26, Vonnie noted that all campers listened to a taped message by Mr. Townsend, general director and co-founder of Wycliffe Bible Translators. In light of coming events, Mr. Townsend's words and choice of Scripture were singularly prophetic and meaningful. On three-by-five-inch ruled notepaper, Vonnie wrote:

Townsend 1–26–55—We have an almost impossible task before us which will require complete dependence on God. Therefore, we must learn to ask God for specific help. We must never forget to ask God for the impossible.

2 Timothy 2:10—We must be strong, not in ourselves but in the power of His might because God calls on the unknown and weak to do His will. Always remember the armor of Ephesians 6.

Vonnie then listed ten points that looked like a special list of Wycliffe ten commandments.

1. A life of prayer and faith will result in a life of production.

2. We must keep humble.

3. We are here to minister to our host country.

4. We must identify with people.

5. We must not be cynical.

6. Always be sympathetic.

7. We should have a burden of love for each other and the ethnic people with whom we work.

8. We are scientists as well as Bible translators.

9. S.I.L. must be known as an organization that is willing to serve all people.

10. S.I.L. cooperates with governments and science.

Two days later Vonnie began to understand some of the practical results of God calling the weak to perform His work. Vonnie, with half her fellow campers, began Jungle Camp's great "canoe hike." The other half, who would go the following week, watched and cheered from the riverbank as their colleagues, four and five in each dugout canoe, rushed through the first white rapids.

Twenty rapids and three upsets later, Vonnie and her companions ended their river voyage at the bottom of a steep canyon gorge in the river. After a supper of soup and corn bread, Vonnie climbed into her jungle hammock and fell asleep to the tattoo of an all-night rain dripping on her canvas canopy.

In the morning, after a time of campfire singing, devotions, hiking, and exploring, the group started back up the river. What took a mere two-and-a-half hours of happy, lighthearted, exciting canoeing the previous afternoon, now took eight exhausting hours of poling, paddling, pulling (hence the name "canoe hike"), and straining to maneuver the heavy twenty- and thirty-foot cedar canoes back through the rapids toward Main Base.

Bone weary and too tired to eat, Vonnie flopped on her bed under her mosquito net as soon as she arrived back at Main Base. In an instant she was asleep. Beside her on the nightstand were her underlined notes from Townsend's message:

2 Corinthians 1:3-5—Difficulties are a blessing in disguise. When we have hardships and trials, it is God

Himself who offers us comfort. And in turn we can help others because God's grace is sufficient for every need.

Vonnie's only unpleasant memory of Jungle Camp was leaving Advance Base. Her natural athletic ability and highly developed curiosity made each project and learning experience pure enjoyment—even being asked to prepare and cook the tail of a yard-long alligator from a nearby lagoon! In addition to long, down-river swims, and hunting (she once shot two fish and a wild turkey), Vonnie's diary showed increasing references to "great times" she was having in prayer and Bible study.

Her diary also revealed her continuing battle with motion sickness—a phenomenon she desperately tried to control during her evacuation flight from Advance Base. On this occasion her concern was more than the discomfort of nausea. Her flight companion was Harry, a fellow camper who was intrigued with Vonnie's athletic ability and winsome personality. Repeatedly people told Vonnie her motion sickness was simply a case of mind over matter. But even though she wanted desperately to make the best possible impression on Harry, Vonnie's stomach wouldn't cooperate. Her April 9 entry read: "Packed and left by plane with Harry. Sick most of the way."

As part of her continued training and experience, Vonnie spent two months after Jungle Camp assisting Wycliffe workers Glenn and Emily Stairs among the sea-fishing Huave Indians of Salina Cruz, Mexico. The Huaves have chosen to build their palm-and-pole huts on a finger-thin sand and palm-fringed peninsula that juts forty miles into the Pacific. Severed by the Tehuantepec River at its base, the three-mile-wide peninsula runs parallel to the mainland. At the extreme southern tip, the peninsula almost touches the S-shaped coastline, thereby creating a great ocean lake.

Vonnie's first view of the Huave village of San Mateo was also her first view of the sea. The tiny doll-like palm-thatched-roof huts, rich blue sky with oversized cotton-ball clouds, and pounding blue green surf, were almost too idyllic for Vonnie's nature-loving instincts.

But along with the picturesque setting and hunts for sea shells, Vonnie faced the hard reality of human suffering and need. Her first week's activity included dispensing medicine for hook- and tapeworms, amoebic dysentery, vitamin deficiency, and pneumonia. She stitched machete cuts, assisted in a breach birth, and treated a bleeding umbilicus.

When Vonnie left Jungle Camp, she expressed her desire to be permanently assigned as soon as possible, giving Brazil and Peru as her preferences. She knew she would go to Peru but underlined Brazil as her first choice in anticipation of Wycliffe sending translation teams there in two or three years. Vonnie also indicated her desire to bypass a third summer at S.I.L. But her June 8 entry confirmed her fears: "Glenn came back with several letters for me. It looks like I'll have to go to Norman. Romans 12 and 13 a great blessing. His will be done."

At the bottom of the page was a sentence that was almost Pauline in character: "Ear infection. Pains me much."

In order for Vonnie to be on time for beginning classes at Norman, she made plans to leave San Mateo immediately. But that night wind-tunnel winds from a Pacific cyclone blew in from the Gulf of Tehuantepec blasting San Mateo and the surrounding coastline. For two full days and nights the cyclone peppered livestock, crops, and homes with heavy explosive rain pellets and flying sand. In its continuing fury, the cyclone swelled the Tehuantepec River and pushed the ocean lake across the low-lying peninsula, sweeping hundreds of cattle and livestock out to sea. Miraculously there was no loss of human life.

Vonnie's entries said simply:

June 9—Cyclone hit village last night. Rained all day. Not able to cross river.

June 10—Still not able to leave. River too high. Roof leaks. Still having a lot of pain in ear.

On Saturday, June 11, the rain stopped and the river receded enough for safe crossing. Vonnie noted her travels from an obscure Indian village in southern Mexico to the sophisticated university community of Norman, Oklahoma.

June 11—Left at 12:00 noon with Glenn, two Huave merchants, and Maria, a friend of the Stairs. Walked an hour, then boarded canoe for another hour to Lake Inferior. Paddled two more hours across lake. After lake crossing, hiked an hour to a village and boarded an ox cart. Arrived in Zapotec Indian town about 9:00 P.M. Spent night there.

June 12—Dried out clothing and left on 2:30 bus for Mexico City.

June 13—Had a good day. All my loose ends tied up. Thankful for warmth and prayers of the girls at the "Kettle." Leave for Laredo early tomorrow.

June 14—Arrived in Laredo at 8:00 P.M. Spent evening
   with two high-school girls I met on bus.
June 15—Traveled all day. Spent time trying to sleep.
June 16—In Dallas from 3:00 to 6:00 P.M. Did a little
   shopping. Got bus. Arrived Norman at midnight in
   middle of great hailstorm.

The storms in Mexico and the one that greeted Vonnie
in Norman seemed symbolic of the personal storms of
confusion, change, and growth that would soon take place.

# 5  Hard Races

June 21—As strange as it seems, I have real peace about being here at Norman. And even though I am lost in Dr. Kenneth Pike's lectures and having trouble with phonetics, I have a greater desire for discipline in study.

Jeremiah 17:5
1 Corinthians 19:20

While her spirit was willing, Vonnie battled her incompatible personality. Discipline was often overshadowed by a restless desire to express her natural talent to be with people.

June 29—Rather lost in Pike's lecture. Just don't know what he's talking about. Had date with Harry. Played tennis 5-1 5-1—lovely time! Dorm party in evening.

July 1—Final in Comanche. Didn't do well but had victory in not being upset.

July 2—Wrote two book reports, studied about one and a half hours, then went to street meeting.

By the middle of the summer Vonnie began to solve her linguistic problems only to fall into the problem of two suitors. Harry regularly played tennis and Ping-Pong with Vonnie but as the summer progressed, Walter Steinkraus, a fellow student, was an ardent observer whenever they played. And Vonnie often found Walt next to her during the noon and evening cafeteria lines. After several days of "happening" to be in the right spot at the right time, he asked Vonnie if they might eat together. Vonnie smiled and said, "Of course!" With his foot in the door, Walt made the most of his opportunity and asked Vonnie if she would attend church with him on Sunday. She said *yes*.

At first Vonnie enjoyed the solicitous attentions of Harry and Walt. She continued to play tennis with Harry and spend her suppers and spare evenings talking with Walt. Although quiet in a crowd and at times unable to clearly express himself, Walt was humorous and attentive, Vonnie found.

By the end of the second week after Walt made his "move," Vonnie discovered two boyfriends impractical. On occasions she found both fellows wanting a date at the same time. After a time of prayer and inner reasoning which she described as confusing, Vonnie invited Harry and Walt to a party to have, as she wrote, "a talk to work out a reasonable solution." When the party ended, it was abundantly clear who had won. Vonnie was escorted back to her dorm on Walt's arm. From that moment, Walt became her constant escort to parties, swimming outings, suppers, and church services.

With the coming of romance came a surprising dedication to her studies.

August 5—Studied about four hours. Sang in a sacred concert in evening, then studied until 2:00 A.M.

August 6—Up at 6:30. A real day of joy and victory in studying. Worked 12 hours on paper for phonemics. Had lunch and supper with Walt.

On the eighteenth, Vonnie noted her studies paid off. "Got a *B* in my Kiowa paper."

Vonnie enjoyed being with Walt but it was not yet clear that he was the one the Lord had for her. After S.I.L. closed in late August, Vonnie made two significant entries:

Such a relief to have papers all complete. Walt helped me pack. Will be traveling with him to Arizona to see his parents.

Was out with Walt until 1:00 A.M. Possibility of us going to field together. It's his desire but I am not certain.

Walt made his overture to Vonnie based on a letter he received a few days earlier from the Wycliffe Board. In two short paragraphs it told him he was accepted as a Wycliffe member and assigned to the Pacific area as requested.

Unlike Vonnie, Walt submitted his character references early, allowing the candidate office time to process his application during the summer. There were two remarks by Wycliffe staff members worthy of comment.

He drove down here in an old Kaiser. This shows either great determination or lack of intelligence!

His linguistic ability is not impressive but satisfactory —*B*+, *C* and *C*+. He is, however, a dogged worker. I strongly recommend him for service with W.B.T.

But the report that best captured Walt's personality came from a former student at Fort Wayne Bible School: "Wally is one of the most determined and diligent fellows I know. He is kind and simple in his mannerisms. He loves our Lord sincerely and earnestly, nor is he ashamed to own Him in a difficult place. Wally is, however, easily embarrassed but very bold in a place that demands courage."

And nothing, judging from Walt's lack of experience with romance, took more courage than that which Vonnie recorded in her August 29 entry:

> Left Norman with Walt at 1:00 P.M. for Prescott, Arizona. Traveled all night. Walt kissed me for the first time!

After meeting Walt's parents, who according to her diary were "very nice," Vonnie left for a short visit to California and Sulphur Springs, Arkansas, before returning to Sheboygan.

Walt's first of many letters to Vonnie was dated September 17, 1955.

Dear Vonnie,

Chances are this may yet get to you in California. I am not really in the mood for writing. My pen is leaking, and my chair is too far from the table—it's round! Besides, it's so nice outdoors; a perfect day to sit around and think Kiowa [one of the languages he and Vonnie studied at S.I.L.].

Trust you had a good trip. California certainly must feel honored to have you there. Flags here were at half-mast after you left.

Will pray you have safe sailing to Sulphur Springs. If you remember and have time, please write. I'll be staying at my brother's place for a couple of weeks then moving to Wheaton to take some courses in Greek. I am looking forward to seeing my brother again.

Your

*Walt*

Vonnie's first letter crossed his and was written after she arrived in Sulphur Springs, Arkansas.

Sunday, September 18

Dear Walt,

It's great to be at this Wycliffe conference. There are people here from all over the world. It's about 10:30. Just got back from a little walk with a couple of girls. Such a lovely night. Crickets are singing and the stars are so beautiful and bright. We are right in the middle of the Ozarks. The scenery is lovely. Wish you were here to enjoy it with me. . . .

Besides writing about people she met and places she visited, Vonnie in this and many of her subsequent letters made pointed references to the number of mutual friends who were getting married. "Oh, by the way, Ernie is engaged to Mary. You remember them from S.I.L."

On her way home from Sulphur Springs, Vonnie stopped overnight in Chicago to meet Walt and his brothers and tell him of receiving her assignment to Peru. Her first letter after she arrived in Sheboygan surprised Walt with something few people knew she practiced.

September 26, 1955

Dear Walt,

It's so good to be back home with my parents. Mom and Dad are well and rejoicing in the Lord. I guess Mom will take it rather hard when I leave. But she is happy the Lord has called me to serve Him.

I have started to fast. It's a problem when I go visiting because people always want to fix me a lunch or snack. I would rather not have people know. This is between the Lord and me. I just feel that for right now it's the Lord's will to spend a few days fasting and praying, especially since I'll be speaking Sunday morning, afternoon, and evening.

I know you are having problems getting support. When I think of getting all my equipment and support for Peru it all seems so impossible. But the Lord has given me real peace. I know I'll be ready when He wants me to go.

I am looking forward to seeing my sister, Phyllis, and her children. They will be coming from Madison this weekend to visit us. My brother-in-law and Dad are going up north for a week of hunting. Daddy just loves the out-of-doors and would like Phyllis and me to come along, but I can't take the time. I did take time out to go to the farm. Had a great time—picked apples, pitched hay, sawed wood, and took a hike.

Mom and Dad are looking forward to meeting you. I hope you can come up some weekend soon. Next week will be very busy as I have many friends to see. Would appreciate your prayers for many of my unsaved friends I'll be seeing.

Love in our Lord,

*Vonnie*

P.S. I'll be in Chicago October 8 for West Sub's alumni meeting. Perhaps we could go to Wheaton's football game.

October 1

Dear Vonnie,

I was happy to find your letter of the 26th when I came in. Was surprised about your fast. I am sure it will be good for you and honoring to our Lord as you experience this fellowship with Him.

Willy and I drove into Chicago yesterday. Went to our church in the morning, a Negro Sunday school in the afternoon, then back to church in the evening. In between time I had a chat with one of the "blue boys on motorcycle." I made a left-hand turn at wrong corner. He was real nice and it was easy to be friendly. He cautioned me about such signs up ahead.

Will be praying for your friends. Looking forward to seeing you on the eighth.

With love,

*Walt*

Vonnie's weekend in Chicago was a happy time for Walt—crisp October air, infectious roars of spirited crowds ablaze with impassioned cheers, and the warmth of Vonnie's soft hands in his.

While Walt seemed to know that Vonnie was all his dreams rolled into one, Vonnie wasn't sure. She enjoyed him but there was the memory of an old childhood flame that still flickered momentarily in her heart. Following the weekend with Walt, she wrote in her diary:

October 10—Called D. It was wonderful to see him.

Vonnie further reminisced about D. and then in a later entry admitted that even though she felt strongly for him, it was not to be. Part of her change in thinking came from Walt's persistent letters.

October 12, 1955

Dear Vonnie,

Almost four days have passed since I last saw you. I hope you won't think it too forward to write today. Looking at it another way you might purposely forget me if I keep putting it off, and you wouldn't want me to have such fears, would you?

Nothing very exciting since you left. If I were to keep a diary, it would go something like this:

Monday—accidentally killed a possum who reversed his field in the middle of the road. In the evening drove to Chicago with Sam and his wife to see the new Moody film, *Time and Eternity*. Really wanted to stay home but I had left my shaving kit at Sam's so it was either go in, or whiskers.

Tuesday—Had a long talk with my house parents. They're so good and like to talk.

Wednesday—Looked for Saturday work. Went to chapel to hear Paul Reese. He's holding special meetings—did me good. I think I'll really miss such spiritual help when I get to the field. After the service went to Sunday school prayer meeting. Came home and thought about you.

Today—Worked at Youngs' clearing yard for landscaping. Then installed electrical finishings. After work ran with the cross-country boys at the golf course. Was good to get out there again with the fellows. Only I didn't think I was so out of condition. Started getting heavy at the first hill. Ate supper. Went to chapel with Willy. Was lonesome so decided to write a line to you.

Love,

*Walt*

P.S. Also had a physical and it looks like I'll have to have an operation for a hernia.

As Walt persisted, Vonnie's letters became more frequent and in each there was an unconscious attempt to bring him up-to-date with meaningful details of her past and present life.

October 13

I certainly did have a lovely weekend with you in Chicago. Especially the nice hike down at the Morton Arboretum. How I love these fall days. Today I took the car and went out to several of our old hiking grounds by the lake and Sheboygan River. It was lovely.

October 17

I went to the club at church last Thursday night. It was such fun. My old girl friends love to talk about our high-school days and the crazy things we did. When I look back I marvel at God's grace in giving me such peace and joy in Him. At one time my happiness was so dependent on people and circumstances.

I have been speaking and showing slides. An uncle and aunt have pledged $75 per year to my support . . . .

Vonnie's letters also showed her unique ability to enter into the joys and sorrows of others.

October 29, 1955

Dear Walt,

It's 7:00 P.M. Spending a quiet evening at home writing letters.

Had a letter from Winnie Christensen, a former classmate of mine at West Sub. Her husband is an announcer on WMBI in Chicago. Winnie has had so much sickness and sorrow recently. But through all this she has such a radiant testimony for the Lord . . . .

A few weeks later, Vonnie had a mixture of joy and frustrated awkwardness when Walt spent a weekend with her, meeting her parents and sister. After he left, Vonnie's mother, in her breezy open manner, shook her head and said, "Well, Vonnie, he sure isn't like your sister's husband. I don't know what you see in him. He's so shy and timid—he can hardly talk!"

Phyllis didn't voice her feelings then but said later, "This little fellow was so unattractive to me that I couldn't understand what Vonnie saw in him. I probably thought this because the contrast between Walt and my own husband was so obvious. My husband Dick is tall, good-looking and an outgoing charmer. But the Lord had a lot to teach me. I discovered later that although Walter didn't display much emotion, you could feel his depth and dedication."

Phyllis was correct in describing Walt as a person who didn't display much emotion. Sometimes he did, however, expose his true feelings in letters.

. . . I'm in a happy mood tonight. Just itching to put my roommate through the wringer. I don't do this every week. First time this year! Perhaps I should hear his side of the story first . . . .

After Walt's visit to Sheboygan, there was a noticeable change in their letters. Words which before only hinted at their feelings now were plain and agonizing, as both struggled to align faithfulness to God's will and committed responsibilities with their exploding feelings.

Vonnie's plane reservation to Peru was set for early January, 1956, and there was yet so much to say and know before time and geography separated them for what seemed would be forever.

November 18, 1955

Dear Walt,

. . . I trust we will be able to spend some time together before we must leave. I have been praying about this. I know it will be hard for both of us when we face the possibility of not seeing each other again. We must pray that our last few hours together will be a time of spiritual blessing; that we might part as stronger Christians.

Isn't it wonderful to know that our Heavenly Father is leading each step of the way? Truly there is nothing I want more than His will for my life.

Saturday, A.M.—Thursday night I stopped in at the church to see Reverend Mooney and his wife. We were discussing youth work and then all of a sudden we were discussing dating, engagement, and marriage. Reverend Mooney does a lot of marriage counseling.

I don't know what he thought, but I got about an hour's lecture. I thought I knew a lot, but found I didn't . . . .

December 12, 1955

Dear Walt,

This morning I spent a long time with the Lord in prayer. It seemed there were so many burdens. For some reason I felt very close to you and asked the Lord to be very precious and near you. When I got your card today telling me your father went to be with the Lord, I realized why I had this burden for you.

Yesterday afternoon, Mom, Dad, and I went out to the farm. They let me off about a mile and a half from the farm and I walked the rest of the way along the lake. It was beautiful—the snow, lake, and air so crisp and wonderfully refreshing. I hiked to our woods along the lake and looked at the evergreens Grandfather planted just before he died. After my hike I met Dad going up the lane and we hiked down one of the gullies and then to the farm. For all I know that might be the last time I will ever hike with my daddy . . . .

The realization of a prolonged separation broke in on Walt late in December during his convalescence from his serious hernia operation.

December 19, 1955

Dear Vonnie,

I hope you can read this. Really haven't had much practice writing letters lying on my back. Will try and get this letter done in a hurry. I might not feel like it later. My trouble is finding a position where the sore doesn't pain. Had a rough time last night until they put me to sleep. But seeing some of the others, I sure ought not to complain. Now I will be able to understand better about other people when they go through this kind of thing.

Later . . . Well, I was interrupted with breakfast, a bath, bedmaking, pills, and what not . . . .

Sure hope you can come down this week. Darling, you may never understand what it would mean to me to see you at this time. If you come, why not call from the station. I could tell you the best way to get out. You have to make several transfers. If it's evening it wouldn't be safe at all. But Willy is working near here in Chicago and gets off early. He could pick you up and bring you down.

Love,

*Walt*

Enclosed in Walt's letter was a check for ten dollars which he said was to "help with the train fare." Vonnie never cashed it. Her heavy speaking schedule and last-minute packing made a trip to Chicago impossible before her January fifth departure for Peru. And Walt's letter didn't arrive until after he had been discharged. She didn't know how deeply he needed her until it was too late.

December 19, 1955

Dear Walt,

It's 9:30 A.M. I have several calls to make and so many details to take care of before I leave. I have three

55 gallon steel barrels almost packed thanks to Dad
and Mom. Dad came home from the office Saturday
and said, "Okay, we're going to get some packing done
this afternoon." I had a hard time keeping up with him!
As always he was patient and sweet. I had asked him
for a few tools and he went to the hardware store and
bought so much for me. Everything from padlocks to
rifle shells, aluminum roofing, hammer, saw, screwdriv-
ers, etc., etc. I am so fearful of guns but he insists on
me taking his 22 rifle along. (I think I'll take it out!)

I am planning to leave for Peru via Miami January
5 on Flight 73 from Midway Airport. I am glad the
trip to Lima is only 24 hours. I get terribly sick on
planes. I was hoping Mom and Dad would take me to
Chicago. But they aren't much for going to Chicago
in winter. Mom had a bad car accident last year and
she's still nervous. They'll be taking me to Milwaukee.
Then I'll get the fast 7:45 A.M. train and should be in
Chicago about 9:05 and can spend the evening with
you and most of the following day after I pick up my
visa and shop for some tapes for Spanish study. I hope
you will be able to meet me then.

Tomorrow is my commissioning service. A few of
my unsaved friends will be there. It's my prayer that
they might realize the reality of Christ and why I am
going to Peru. I'll see you soon.

Love,

*Vonnie*

Vonnie plainly loved Walt and her love grew stronger
week by week. Yet she ended her letter with a verse
from Philippians 3:13 and 14 which she hoped would

ease the hurt of separation and somehow show she was subject to a higher will.

. . . forgetting those things which are behind, and reaching forth unto those things which are before, I press toward the mark for the prize of the high calling of God in Christ Jesus.

# 6 City of Kings

It wasn't possible. How could anyone know her love for flowers? Yet there she was, standing in Lima's cramped overcrowded air terminal with a dozen and a half long-stemmed roses in her hands.

Vonnie didn't know it then, but Mrs. Cudney, house-mother for Wycliffe's guest home in Lima, makes it her mission to greet each new worker with a bouquet of roses. Warm and effervescent, Mrs. Cudney is the undisputed entrepreneur of culinary arts, unofficial protocol officer in matters of dress and Latin American courtesy, and walking encyclopedia on everything from the finest restaurants to best buys on Peruvian artifacts, clothing, pots, and pans.

In the short eight-mile drive from the airport to the handsome Wycliffe guest home, Mrs. Cudney and Vonnie became instant friends. Both discovered their mutual love of flowers and animals. "People tease me for the way I collect animals," said Mrs. Cudney. "I do have to admit the back patio sometimes looks like a little zoo. But it's so easy and natural to pick up animals from our jungle base at Yarinacocha. Just wait till you go there!"

As they drove and talked, Mrs. Cudney sensed that

Vonnie was a person who might need to be reminded about the differences between Lima and Sheboygan. "You'll find the people of Lima warm and friendly," said Mrs. Cudney. "But be careful of the men. This is Latin America! And by all means be careful of your purse."

Vonnie laughed to herself when she heard the word *purse*. She remembered her phone call to Winnie Christensen just before leaving for Miami to see if she had left her purse there. Winnie's exasperated, "How can you be so calm about losing your passport and visa just before you are leaving?" still rang in her ears. She must write Winnie right away and tell her she found it.

"As you know," said Mrs. Cudney, interrupting Vonnie's thoughts, "you will start Spanish study in the morning. And when we can make arrangements, you and another girl will live with a Peruvian family. This is an enjoyable way of getting to know Lima and Spanish culture."

Vonnie knew she would enjoy meeting new people. But the city of Lima, built by Francisco Pizarro, Peru's sixty-two-year-old conqueror in 1535, was another matter. All Vonnie could see was mile after mile of roofless shacks in the most sickly slum conditions she had ever seen. It wasn't until much later that she discovered Lima's palm-lined boulevards, fashionable suburbs, skyscrapers, and sophisticated cosmopolitan atmosphere. And then she knew why Lima meant "City of Kings."

The following morning Vonnie began an extensive series of letters to Walt. And as always, she began her letters with what time it was, never seeming to know the exact time.

Thursday, January 11

Dear Walt,

It's about 6:30 A.M. I'm writing this in bed. The other girls are still sleeping so I'll try to be quiet for a little while. I arrived last night about 8:15 P.M. Three Wycliffe girls from the guest home, Mrs. Cudney, and Cecil Hawkins were there to meet me. Mrs. Cudney gave me a huge bouquet of talisman roses. Cecil took care of getting me through customs. It's been wonderful so far. The guest home is lovely and there are beautiful flowers in the yard.

Just as soon as I have my devotions and breakfast I'll be off to Spanish class. They started Monday which means I'll be busy catching up. Do pray I will grasp Spanish quickly so I'll be able to speak to the people. One of the girls I met at S.I.L. last summer and I will be moving out in a few days to live with a Peruvian family. This will help us get into the language much faster.

The flight to Miami was wonderful. I wasn't a bit dizzy. When I arrived I took out insurance and called Lima to let them know when I would arrive. I'm glad I did. It was wonderful to be met.

On the flight to Lima I really got to know one of the Peruvian stewardesses. She knew a little English and I knew a little Spanish so we got along fine. I invited her to visit the guest home and plan to write her.

I am so glad we had a few extra days together before I left. I guess we really got to know each other better. Do pray we will always want His will and that He will continue to prepare us for what is ahead. I am going to miss you. After Monday night I felt closer to you than ever before. I know being away from you is going to be hard. I know also I must be more dependent on the Lord. I want always to be submissive to His will.

Do write often. I'll be awfully busy and won't be able to write as often as I would like but I will be praying and remembering you.

Love in Him,

*Vonnie*

In the afterglow of her commissioning service, friends wishing her Godspeed, and the wonder of high service for God in new surroundings, the hard realities of life seemed nonexistent. But Vonnie's January 14 letter to Walt showed she had no illusions about this continuing.

Dear Walt,

It's about 7:00 P.M. My roommate is writing letters in the study. I've been resting all afternoon as I haven't been feeling too well. I got sick after visiting the Inca ruins outside of Lima. I came home and decided to rest. I didn't go down for dinner and Mrs. Cudney was concerned. She brought some water and fruit juice and a little pillow. Our beds are very hard with thin straw mattresses. The pillows are huge and also filled with straw. We never use them. But considering everything, we sleep well, probably because we're so tired at the end of the day. It's hard work trying to understand what people are talking about when you can't understand the language.

Along with reading *Beyond Humiliation* by J. G. Mantle, I have been reading *Home, Courtship, Mar-*

*riage, and Children* by J. R. Rice. My roommate went
up in smoke when she saw the book. I guess she dis-
agrees with him about 80 percent and I agree with him
about 80 percent! We had quite a discussion!

My roommate and I are different as night and day.
After meeting her at S.I.L. I feared that of all the
girls in Wycliffe she would be the only one I would
have difficulty getting along with. When I came here
and found I would have to live with her, I was upset.
But I have taken it as from the Lord and have really
prayed for the Lord to give me love for her no matter
how she acts. I do wish you would pray for her, too.
The Lord has given me an attitude of not being offended but I don't know how a non-Christian might
react to some of the things she says. She gets irritated
at little things like crowded buses, people bumping
her, crying children, doors slamming, etc., etc. I don't
want to be critical because in many ways she is a
dear and so considerate. Pray the Lord will teach me
all He has for each of us during the next two months
of language study. I'm thankful you aren't irritated
easily!

You'll be thinking about leaving for Jungle Camp
soon. Kind of wish I was going along at the same time.
But I know the Lord would have it this way for now.

Love in our Lord,

*Vonnie*

Philippians 3


According to Vonnie's January 17 letter, her prayers
for a better understanding between her roommate and
her were answered.

Dear Walt,

It's about 7:15 P.M. The girls have gone to supper. They just brought me a letter from home. I felt rather lonely today. Hoped I would hear from you. I have been terribly sick but I guess the worst is over. My temperature is coming down and I hope soon to go back to classes. We had planned to move in with a Peruvian family today but will probably move in next week.

It's hard to understand why I should get so sick. Perhaps the weeks of little sleep, emotional stress, leaving home, new climate, and food, have all had a part in making me ill. I guess the Lord knew I needed a rest and this was the only way to get one!

I feel terrible about getting behind in my Spanish study, but there's nothing I can do about it. I started to get sick on Thursday with a terrible headache, then abdominal pains, soreness in my bones and joints. My tonsils have been sore and bleeding and I have been sleeping constantly for the past two days. I was up last night for a few minutes and fainted. I guess I need more rest. My roommate and others have been so dear to me. I've always hated to be waited on but can't tell you how much their kindness and thoughtfulness have meant to me. Times like this bring about a real deep love for each other. I know it has drawn me very close to my roommate and our problems seem never to have existed.

I suppose you have heard about the five men who were killed by the Aucas in Ecuador. One of the fellows was Rachel Saint's brother. And perhaps you remember Ed McCully and Jim Elliott from Wheaton. We're crushed and yet can't feel it as deeply as their wives and those who knew them personally. One of the girls here worked closely with two or three of the couples and when she heard the news cried for hours. She is burdened for the work that is left behind. There seem to be so few men to do God's work on the mission field and now these five taken all at once. I pray many young people will be stirred and willing to go.

Do write soon and don't tell my folks I have been sick. I'll be fine in a couple of days. Hoping to hear from you soon.

Love in our Lord,

*Vonnie*

Walt's response to Vonnie's letter was short and seemed to lack the full depth of love Vonnie was experiencing for him.

1/13/56
Wheaton

Dear Vonnie,

Seems such a long time since last I saw you on the plane. Have been thinking a lot about you and will always be looking forward to your letters.

Just finished listening to a recording of another report from HCJB. Our campus here certainly has been sobered by the Auca killings. Our prayers are for their loved ones and the Aucas. I am sure this will be a victory for Christ in reaching this tribe. Trusting many will be challenged to go. Makes one wish he were already going out.

I found your earring. Will mail it to you along with your books today. I have to go to work now but will write again. I'm praying for you every day. We also prayed for you in the world prayer group. Have so much to do before I leave for Jungle Camp. Pray that my time will be used wisely.

Love,

*Walt*

Saturday, January 21

Dear Walt,

I received your letter of January 13 this morning. It was good to hear from you. Just got back from the beach with my roommate. It was wonderful to have a free day. Oh, I guess I didn't mention that we have moved to our Peruvian home. The Ponces are wonderfully kind and hospitable. They've taken us in as their very own. They have four daughters—21, 19, 17, and 15. They seem to be truly sweet and we have wonderful times together. This morning we went to the market and tonight we are going riding with the family. Tomorrow we are going to church.

This afternoon we had dinner at the guest home, then went to the beach. It was a bit breezy but very refreshing. A few of the girls got stung by jellyfish. There seem to be an abundance of them here. I had a most interesting time climbing and crawling through a few narrow crevices in the rocks. You know my adventurous spirit!

Yesterday I got up about 5:30 for study and devotions. I am enjoying my new family very much and already feel quite at home. The difficulty of adjusting to new people and culture is not as bad as I thought. The food is wonderful, but almost too much. We have lunch about 2:00 P.M. which usually starts with a heavy vegetable soup. Sometimes it has an egg in it.

Then we have potatoes or rice, a big green salad, chicken, duck, or beef, and dishes of string beans, lentils, carrots, or eggplant. My poor mother would just die if she saw what we eat. She and Dad are careful about eating the right kinds of health and natural foods. I don't know how the Peruvians can eat so much. I try to eat as much as I can because I don't want to offend. I only wish the portions were smaller! At least we seldom have a dessert after the meal. If we do, it's usually a banana, orange, or piece of papaya.

We will be here until the end of March and then I will go to the branch conference at the base at Yarinacocha. Do continue to pray I might grasp all the Lord has for me. There are so many things to learn and so little time.

I miss you very much and remember you in my prayers. It is my constant prayer that during these months of separation we will be drawn closer to the Lord and, if it is His will, to one another. I know it will be hard if we are never permitted to see each other again. And yet we know His will is perfect and even during times of separation the Lord is able to make each of us more conformable to Himself. I am anxious for the future but perhaps it is better that we do not know.

Love,

*Vonnie*

Vonnie was continually impressed with the way Wycliffe's Peru branch concerned itself with maintaining a witness both to the Indians and government officials. "I just received my official registration papers," she wrote, "and am now an official resident of Peru. I'm thankful we cooperate with the government and have a burden and love for those in authority."

Perhaps the biggest and newest difference for Vonnie was experiencing the ache and pain of wanting to be with Walt. "There are times," she wrote, "when I so want to share a burden with you or long for you to hold me." And then as if her emotions were made content by being able to write what she felt inside, Vonnie was again caught up in the expectancy of her new assignment.

March 5

Dear Walt,

It's about 5:30 P.M. I have been busy writing letters, working on my prayer letter, and practicing my piano accordion. By the way, my barrels arrived last week. Everything seems to be okay, although I haven't unpacked anything except my accordion. One of the barrels got banged up. I'm thankful my accordion didn't get damaged. I was worrying about that.

I'll be shipping these over to Yarinacocha in about two weeks. Did I mention we have our last Spanish class on March 23 and leave by plane for the base on the 28th? I'm looking forward to working with Dr. Eichenberger in the clinic.

Oh, by the way, I started taking accordion lessons last Wednesday with one of the other girls. Our teacher speaks only Spanish so it's interesting. I have learned a lot of Spanish here in Peru, much more than in my time in Mexico. Wish I could have studied longer. Some of the students are having a rough time. My Spanish study at Wheaton and the linguistics at S.I.L. have really helped.

It's been a week since I last heard from you but I suppose you are awfully busy at Jungle Camp. Just think—it has been eight weeks since we last saw each other. By the way, I received the earring and little track shoe you sent. I put the track shoe on a gold chain and have been wearing it.

The Ponces are always asking about you—questions, questions, questions! If you have a picture, you must send it so they can see what you look like. They say I am looking better every day. I've gained about three pounds which makes me rather unhappy. But if I eat less I know it would offend them. My hair is a shade lighter and longer. My skin is about three shades darker. I really have a nice tan. Perhaps you wouldn't recognize me!

The Ponces invited us to a party last Saturday night. We had a nice time but I had an upset stomach yesterday. They served sandwiches with the weirdest combinations—fish, eggs, cheese, all mixed up together!

I got such a sweet letter from my sister and one from Mom and Dad. Two of my friends and their husbands have been coming over for Bible study with Dad and Mom. This is another wonderful answer to prayer.

I trust you are having a wonderful time at Jungle Camp and that the Lord is teaching you many new things. Jungle Camp was a great spiritual blessing to me.

Love,

*Vonnie*

P.S. We have been studying Hebrews on Tuesday evenings at the guest home. Hebrews 12:1-7.

Walt responded to Vonnie's letter with a description of what he was doing and learning at Jungle Camp's Main Base. And he, like Vonnie, focused on the canoe overnight hike. "We got rather soaked going down the rapids," he wrote, "but sure had fun." With an elaborate description of how he had become sick during the overnight but was now well, Walt ended with, "Excitement, excitement! One of the girl campers discovered a large tarantula in her shoe!"

Vonnie enjoyed Walt's comment about the tarantula and in her next letter topped it with a story of her own. The origins seemed more appropriate to a high-school locker room than a Peruvian home where two missionary women were living.

While she was exploring a nearby island on an outing with a group of church young people, one of her Peruvian friends caught a little chameleon and gave it to her. She wrote:

> . . . I put it in my earring case and took it home. In the morning while my roommate was getting dressed, I got out my case and was going to take a picture of it outside in the garden, then let it go. But while I was getting it out, it sprang out of my hand and ran away. At first I thought it was in the closet but I couldn't find it. When I started to leave, my roommate grabbed my arms, started to twist them, pinned me against the wall, and gave me a terrible tongue lashing. I knew if I talked back she would slap my face so I just prayed the Ponces wouldn't hear her.
>
> After that she felt terrible and apologized and we had prayer together. She recognizes her problem with tem-

per and says it seems to be getting worse. When we first lived together I felt badly about it but after a while I got used to being told to keep still, shut up, etc. For me to be hurt or offended would be my own pride. It's been hard for me because I know this is displeasing to the Lord. I pray for her every day and have been trying to avoid arguments. I do want to help her and I know the Lord has much to teach me from this.

Vonnie's collision with her roommate caused her to reveal both to herself and Walt something she had before been unwilling to admit. In the same letter she wrote:

I marvel at the way the Lord has and is changing my attitude. When I came back from Mexico after living with and seeing married people, I was thankful to be single. I felt children were too great a responsibility. I thought also the Lord was showing me that being a wife and mother was not for me. But now I've changed and I trust my change of heart is from the Lord and not my own desires. Our hearts can be so deceitful and I want only His will because I know we would never be happy together unless we were perfectly convinced in our minds and had peace in our hearts that we were meant for each other.

The Lord has become precious to me and I know His love is sufficient. Yet to have someone love me has been very wonderful. At times I wish I wasn't so human. The Lord must always be our first love. In the past, other desires and things have taken first place in my life. James 4:14 really hit me. How short our lives are in comparison with eternity! There is so much to be done and so little time remains. I am praying for a balanced life and don't want to waste time on things that do not have eternal value. I'm afraid I am still far from that.

Love,

*Vonnie*

P.S. My next letter will be from Yarinacocha.

1 Peter 1:18-25
Psalm 37:4, 5

To arrive at Yarinacocha, Wycliffe's Peruvian jungle base, Vonnie flew two hours over the Andes in the non-pressurized cabin of a commercial airplane. At the appropriate moment during the flight, stewardesses passed out specially designed rubber tubes which supplied extra oxygen to sustain the passengers in the high altitude. "It was too cloudy to see much," she wrote. "Just a few peaks poking up through the clouds."

Vonnie then landed at Pucallpa, a raw lumbering town of about 3,000 that sits on the edge of the Ucayali River like a festered sore. With open sewers, red rutted clay streets and great balsa logs laying around like scattered Tinker Toys, Vonnie had only one comment. "The heat hit me like a lead balloon. I feel like a wilted daisy. Still I trust I will in time get accustomed to the heat and humidity."

In a truck from Pucallpa, Vonnie bumped, splashed, and rolled over four and a half miles of mud and potholes on the Transandean Highway to reach the cutoff road that would take them to Yarinacocha. "The base is lovely," she wrote. "Most of the families have their own homes. It seems strange to see houses, plane hangars, administrative buildings and a radio tower way out here in the jungle. But having a base like this in the middle of Amazonia seems the only way to reach the thirty or so tribes here. I'll tell you more about the base when I have seen everything."

In the morning Vonnie added a P.S. to her letter. "I couldn't sleep last night. It was so hot and little bugs kept biting me. Just came in from a half-hour hike by the lake. Took pictures of some little Indian girls swimming. They were so cute. Lake Yarina is beautiful—fifteen miles long and about two miles wide. Our base is built along one side of it. Now if you were here we could go canoeing! But you aren't, so I can only think about it. 'Bye again."

Vonnie spent the next few days unpacking, getting acquainted with her surroundings and new job. Because extra people were needed to prepare for the branch conference, Vonnie was asked to help in one of the administrative offices. On April 1, Easter Sunday morning, she wrote Walt how particularly blessed she was with Dr. Kenneth Pike's messages.

At Norman, Vonnie never fully understood or felt at ease with Wycliffe's famous linguist. When she saw him on the volleyball court or at the blackboard, his lean, wiry, six-foot, 145-pound frame seemed to erupt with the snap and crackle of escaping electricity. But now she saw him in a different light. This intense, sometimes frightening man brought to the Scriptures the same energy, devotion, and scholarship as he did to his teaching and linguistic theory. She wrote to Walt:

. . . We have had the greatest blessing ever from Dr. Pike. (He is here in Peru for a special linguistic workshop and to see about getting S.I.L. into Brazil.) His devotional messages dealt in a practical way with our interpersonal relationships with fellow Christians. As you know, I was troubled about my relationship with my roommate and have been trying to discover what the Lord wanted to teach me. The messages have helped me to understand my roommate better. Over the years the Lord has taught me much from the people I have roomed with. The lessons learned from my roommate while living with the Ponces have been the most diffi- cult. But how precious it is now. I have also come to understand I should be more faithful in my letter writ- ing. There are several people back home that I have been burdened about but never seem to get time to write. One of these has been one of my dearest friends who has drifted from the Lord. I started to write sev- eral times but ended up throwing them away. I feel badly about this. Somehow I can already feel the pain she is going to experience when she again recognizes how much the Lord loves her. And I feel badly knowing how much the Lord has been grieved.

On April 2, sparked by an interview with Harold Goodall, at that time the director of the Peru branch, Vonnie wrote the most pointed of her many letters.

. . . On Friday I had a conference with Harold Good- all. He wanted to know if I had thought about selecting a partner and if I had a particular interest in a tribe. I was a little hesitant. I suppose he wondered what my problem was. He then asked about us. I had talked to him about you when I saw him in Sulphur Springs. He wanted to know if there was anything definite.

How do you feel about our relationship? Has the

Lord ever given you anything definite from His Word concerning the future? I hope you will always be honest in telling me how you feel. I often wonder if my change of attitude toward marriage is completely of the Lord. I want it to be. There is so much I don't understand. Perhaps I am too impatient in wanting to know what the future has for us. Then again there might be a purpose in wanting to know. One of my girl friends from California wrote telling me she was concerned about our future and has been praying the Lord will show us His will. Will you write soon and let me know what you think? I'll be anxiously waiting for your reply.

Love in Him,

*Vonnie*

Hebrews 12:1-33

# 7 *God Knows Best*

Today, the clinic at Yarinacocha has three doctors, a dentist, seven nurses, and a highly developed community health program. But in April, 1956, the small two-bed clinic, which later became a general store, had Dr. Eichenberger, Vonnie, and two other nurses.

During the mornings Dr. Eichenberger treated seventy or more outpatients. The afternoons were reserved for attending to the health needs of Wycliffe workers, research, and technical writing. He was a natural teacher and wasted no time introducing Vonnie to the different responsibilities she would be expected to handle.

Vonnie began vaccinating and treating Indians for whooping cough, tetanus, typhoid, malaria, and many other tropical ailments. In addition she taught the concepts of health, hygiene, and child welfare. While Vonnie found her new assignment exciting and rewarding, she continued to struggle with the outcome of her future with Walt and the added conflict of wanting to work in a tribal area.

Sunday, April 15

Dear Walt,

. . . I started working in the clinic on Thursday. Since then I have heard the rumor that they would like me to work here at the base for the next year. Our regular nurse is due for furlough in July. I feel that some tribal experience would be valuable but the decision is in the Lord's hands. But whatever my temporary assignment is, I know it will be what I need most.

On Wednesday and Thursday we had a bad storm and the trails became very slippery. Thursday afternoon Doc asked me to go with him to visit a sick Piro Indian who had pneumonia. It was a long hike. Glad I like this sort of thing! On the way home my toe started to ache and by evening it was throbbing. I went to bed early and woke up during the night in great pain. Often when I wake up in the night I feel led to pray for some friend. I prayed and asked the Lord to take away the pain.

And a wonderful thing happened! In about ten minutes the pain was gone and I was able to go back to sleep! I praise the Lord for His wonderful love and interest in little insignificant things . . . .

For all Vonnie's growing sensitivity to the Lord's working in her life, she still showed her humanness.

. . . There were so many people and there was so much activity during conference that I am glad it's over. Last night I felt like being by myself for a while. I guess I was a bit depressed. Probably the thought of staying at the base while all my friends go to tribes.

Oh, before I forget, we just heard an encouraging letter from Uncle Cam Townsend about the possibility of S.I.L. going into Russia to work with some of the languages in Siberia. Isn't that wonderful?

April 22

Dear Walt,

It's about 7:15 P.M. and the evening service begins at 7:30. (I'll be giving my testimony.) I've been physically overtired since being here. I think it's the heat and humidity.

Tariri, a Shapra chief, has been having many trials. You probably remember last August he was shot. One of the girls was telling me how the Lord miraculously spared his life. The bullet went through his body only three inches from his heart. He has completely recovered but last week we heard that his home and all his possessions were burned. How much some of these dear Indian believers have suffered for their faith!

I was thrilled this morning to meet an Indian friend of Esther Matteson's. He is a new believer, about a year old in the Lord. Such a brilliant man! Speaks four Indian languages plus Spanish. He was sold as a slave when he was eleven and found the Lord through a Piro Indian evangelist using the translated Scriptures. He is such a friendly person, desirous of studying God's Word and taking the gospel back to his own people . . . .

April 23

Mail goes out tomorrow so will add a little more. Had another busy day in the clinic. Doc is wonderful. I enjoy working with him. I went swimming in the late afternoon. Feel I need the exercise and it's so relaxing. I still tire out fast.

Just think, two more months and you'll be studying

your second year at Norman. I don't envy you at all. What a struggle it was for me! I'll be praying for you. I was so thankful there were friends back home praying for me last summer. Their prayers and my hard studying got me through!

I moved into my own room yesterday in the girls' dorm. It's quite nice. I hope I can stay put for a while. This is the fifth move in four months . . . .

To keep her mind occupied while waiting to hear from Walt, Vonnie took a deeper interest in her work and learned all she could about tropical diseases. "Doc has been wonderfully patient with me," she wrote Walt. "Today he took a great deal of time to explain about various fungus infections." Vonnie concluded with a note about four more Wycliffe children and an Indian language helper coming down with mumps. She also told Walt that she now had peace about her base assignment. She enjoyed her work and gave praise to the Lord for answering her prayers. In later years she would tell how gracious the Lord was for giving her this change of attitude because on May 2 she received her first of several jolts that caused her to rely heavily on what the Lord had been doing for her.

April 20-29

Dear Vonnie,

Seems a long time since the mail plane brought us advance-base campers any mail. About a week, I think. Have my mud stove finished and am getting things ready to make pancakes tomorrow. Last time I tried to make them they all turned out flat!

Just reread your letter of April 2 concerning us. It would be easier if we were closer together and could talk and pray about these things. Our future is still a problem for me. Last summer at Norman I was sure it would work out. Later as we talked about you going to Peru and my interest in the South Pacific, I didn't know what to think. When there were long periods when we didn't see each other and had to write, I began to doubt. Then when we would come together again I would become hopeful.

Now that we are far apart, the problem seems as big as ever. I still have summer school and deputation ahead of me, and you are ready to begin work in a tribe.

Our calling to His work and the limited time we have to do it is such a sacred trust that it would be tragic on my part to ask you to wait for me. And if you did start to work in a tribe, either you or your partner would have to change. That would seem like a waste of time.

Other questions also come. Will we be happy? Do we really love each other? Is marriage a waste of time?

The Lord gave me a verse that is very helpful. "I have taught thee in the way of wisdom; I have led thee in right paths. When thou goest, thy steps shall not be straitened; and when thou runnest, thou shalt not stumble" (Proverbs 4:11, 12).

As I look back and see how wonderfully the Lord has led in my own life I know the future is just as sure and wonderful.

Do share with me your thoughts about all this. I can still see you on that plane and wish I could be with you! Mail is leaving, so till then,

Love,

*Walt*

May 2

Dear Walt,

I received your letter of April 20 today. There is trouble in Lima—something about the army and navy taking over—so there hasn't been mail for over a week. I trust things will get back to normal soon and we can have our regular mail service restored.

The mail came when I was in the clinic. In between patients I read yours. I usually read your letters several times so I won't miss anything.

I have been feeling much better these past few days. At first I thought my tiredness was a spiritual battle and decided to spend more time in prayer. Then last Thursday, Beth, the other nurse, took my blood count and it was way down. I started taking vitamins and iron and already I feel much better. Also bought a can of powdered Nido milk to drink. Our diet lacks calcium. I've only had eggs twice since coming here. I trust I'll soon be feeling as good as new!

Thank you so much for sharing your thoughts concerning our relationship. I suppose you thought I was rather blunt but I feel better now that I know how you feel. I have had wonderful peace these last few days about being here. The way I feel now I wouldn't want to be any other place.

It is true that the Lord has given us a sacred trust. But I don't think it would be tragic for me to wait for you if the Lord wants us to serve Him together. In fact, I feel the Lord has much to teach me during this time of separation. God only does what's best for us. I know the Lord has led in each step of my life and I'm confident that I am right where He wants me to be. But doubts still creep in. I keep feeling it would be nice to know for sure. Perhaps we should pray together at a definite time for a definite answer.

When I look at our situation it seems to be of the Lord. When I doubt it is usually caused by selfish motives. I look at some of the difficult children on the base and think of the burden and heartache I caused my parents and get rather frightened. Children are such a responsibility and I would want nothing but for ours to grow up and serve the Lord. I know this is possible only as our relationship is completely centered in the Lord's love so our lives together will be an example of Christ's love.

When I see friction between husband and wife it scares me. When I think of going to a tribe and being the only Christians surrounded by the power of Satan, we must know deeply in our hearts that Christ has sent us there together. Above everything else, the tribespeople must see Christ through us. A marriage that shows true love and concern between husband and wife can be a powerful influence for good in a heathen culture.

Vonnie's next words were brave and valiant, but her later diary revealed she would remember them through hard tears.

If the Lord meant me for you, I want nothing else. And if the Lord has someone else for you, I will accept this as the Lord's will. I settled the problem of being married or remaining single several years ago. I know His grace is sufficient and His love is all I need. If the Lord wants me married, I only want the man the Lord has chosen for me.

Often in the past my choices have been wrong and the

older I get the more I realize that He knows what's best
for His children. Sometimes it takes me a long time to
accept His will. But He is patient and in the end I
always realize I don't want it any other way.

It was His desire that I be a nurse. It was His desire
that I join W.B.T. and come to Peru. And I have the
assurance that all things will work out for His glory. In
the meantime I continue to pray that the Lord will
soon show us definitely how we can plan our future
together . . . .

May 4

Dear Walter,

It's about 6:30 P.M. I am going to try and finish this
letter before going to breakfast. I had a very busy day
yesterday. I was in the clinic from 7:30 A.M. to 8:00 P.M.
One of our missionary wives had her baby and had a
difficult time. I was with her all day. It's nice our mothers
can have their babies here at the clinic. Doc is capable
in so many fields of medicine. He allows the fathers to
be here for the deliveries, which I think is very nice.
When this mother was having so much pain, the husband said, "This should discourage any single girl from
wanting to get married!" But Beth and I both agree it
would take more than that to discourage us! I have
assisted with so many deliveries and each time I think
perhaps this will someday be me.

It's time for breakfast. All for now. Always remembering you in my prayers.

Love,

*Vonnie*

Joel 2:21   "Fear not . . . be glad and rejoice:
for the Lord will do great things."

During May and most of June, Vonnie's letters to Walt were chatty, buoyant, and free from the deep concern she had previously expressed about their future. She told about her growing fellowship with Beth and the other single girls and frequently mentioned her concern for people back home to become involved in Bible translation.

> . . . A visiting pastor spoke last Sunday evening and told that as he flew over the vast jungle the Lord seemed to burden him for the many tribespeople who have never heard the gospel. As he spoke I became so burdened for the young people back home that I wanted to leave the meeting and pray they would become serious about serving the Lord. So many seem to waste their lives on pursuits that will never count for eternity.

When she wasn't making points about her many friends who were getting engaged, married, or were now seeing or writing to each other, Vonnie talked about the things that happened at the clinic.

> . . . We had another busy week at the clinic. Not quite so many patients—about seventy-five on Monday. Did I tell you about the boy that came in after being sick for a month? We thought it was typhoid. He was full of sores, semiconscious, feverish, and swollen. Doc felt the boy had little chance to live since he seemed to have other complications plus pneumonia. That happened a week ago. The Doc gave him some medicine and vitamin drops and they left. Yesterday his mother brought him back. What a changed little boy! He was alert, breathing normally, and most of the swelling was

gone. It was thrilling to see how the Lord spared his life. It's at times like this that I'm thankful for my work.

This morning we received word on the two-way radio that eight schoolchildren from the Machiguenga tribe died and eight more were very sick. The Indian school-teacher had been trained at the base bilingual school. I understand when the children came out of the jungles to the village where the translator and teacher lived, they were very fearful. Then the epidemic struck. Most believed they became sick because they came out to the village. Now they have been frightened off and gone back to the jungle. It's sad because it was such a battle to get the school started. It makes me realize that we should be more in prayer for these schoolchildren and Christian teachers. People at home need to know how much is involved in getting the Word to those that are without the Lord. . . .

June 18

Dear Walt,

I have been thinking about you this past week as you drive to Norman. Perhaps you are there by now. It's kind of nice to get there a few days early. I never will forget how I felt when I pulled into Norman after six days of traveling alone from Juchitán, Mexico, by bus and sick most of the way. What an ordeal that was!

Yesterday I put my little stove together. The pipe got bent on the way down to Peru and it leaks a bit. This morning I woke to find the stove in a pool of kero-sene. I'm not too happy with it. It takes about forty-five minutes to boil a half pan of water. I am hoping to buy a little Swedish camp stove. It sure pays to have good equipment down here.

Tomorrow I'll be alone in the clinic. I do wish you would pray that the Lord will give me physical strength and wisdom for this increased responsibility. Doc leaves on the 25th for vacation. Beth will be leaving on furlough and I don't know when Lynn will be back. I feel so helpless because of my limited Spanish. I'll be starting Spanish classes again this summer. A teacher from Seattle Pacific College is coming down to do the teaching.

Speaking about Doc and Beth, they never wear watches. Doc has no concept of time, especially when he starts talking! I guess that's one reason why I like working with him. He enjoys visiting with the people of the area and is concerned about their spiritual as well as physical lives.

I was sorry to hear of your illness while you were in the tribe in Mexico. Sounded like the same thing you had on your canoe hike. Do you think it was malaria? You will take care of yourself, won't you? I don't want you to be sick this summer at Norman when you have so many difficult studies.

Got a letter from a girl friend in Bolivia. Her partner came down with hepatitis. We have two more here at the base that came down with it this week. It certainly is a terrible disease and so many of our people come down with it.

It was just a year ago June 11 that I left the tribe in Mexico for S.I.L. It has been interesting to look back over my diary. So much has happened during this past year. Wonder what another year will bring forth. Just think, it has been five months since we were last together. Time is going faster than I thought it would.

Love and my prayers always,

*Vonnie*

James 1:1-6

Sunday, June 24

Dear Walt,

I was up about 5:45 A.M. and took a little walk
after breakfast. In the afternoon I started reading Dr.
Erdman's book, *Storms and Starlight*. I don't know
why, but all of a sudden I felt so alone. Then I read
the verse in the flyleaf of a book my Little Sister from
West Sub gave me—Joshua 1:5b: "I will be with thee:
I will not fail thee, nor forsake thee."

After reading that, the Lord gave me such peace
and joy in knowing He will never leave me. What a
privilege for us to have God's Word when so many
thousands are without it!

Must close now. I miss you.

Love,

*Vonnie*

Vonnie's July 1 and 4 letters displayed her continuing involvement with the spiritual and physical needs of
others.

. . . It's wonderful that you are enjoying your studies.
I know this last year at S.I.L. won't be as hard for
you as it was for me. I never will forget the night last
summer when I tried to stay up all night to get my
reports completed. I worked till 3:00 A.M., then ran
out of paper. Another time the Lord convicted me of
the long hours of study through Psalm 127:2: "It is
vain for you to rise up early, to sit up late, to eat the
bread of sorrows: for so he giveth his beloved sleep."
I was physically tired and didn't feel like studying.
Then I prayed for ten to fifteen minutes during each
hour of study and asked the Lord to help me finish

the paper. It wasn't because I wanted to complete the paper—by this time I almost hated struggling with verb classes. I asked the Lord to help me complete the paper because I knew it was His will.

I can now thank the Lord for such experiences. I always want to be doing things I know are His will but still have much to learn.

July 4

Dear Walt,

I have been thinking about you today and wondering what you are doing. Can't help but remember our first time together. A whole year has passed since then.

Had a long day in the clinic. Just as I was about to leave I had to put hot compresses on a little fellow. Still can't figure out what he had. I think it was a big carbuncle about three inches in diameter. I felt sorry for the little guy. They brought him in a wheelbarrow. There always seems to be something happening in the clinic!

The other day a man asked if we could come to see his brother's wife. She was expecting and had been hemorrhaging for three days. Lynn and I gathered up some things and took the jeep to a little village several miles away. When we got there we saw three midwives who were too upset to give us much information. The poor mother was pale and having great pain. We decided she needed to go to the hospital in Pucallpa so drove back to the base to pick up a truck, cot, and one of the men to help us. When we arrived at the hospital and went to get help, one of the midwives who had come along for the ride ran after me and called me back to the truck. I found the baby arriving, a stillbirth, and immediately started artificial respiration. Soon after a doctor came and began to wash the baby but there was no sign of life even after giving her adrenalin.

We finally got the mother in the hospital. She talked to me about being hungry so I got her something to eat and stayed with her awhile. I left to find the father and relatives to have them give blood. When I found the father I told him about the condition of his wife and went back to the base.

The next morning I discovered that when the father arrived at the hospital, his wife had already died. It was a great shock to all of us but we had brought the matter before the Lord and knew we had done everything we could for her.

I praise the Lord for the peace and calmness He gave me. All day I knew He was going before me and I knew that whatever happened was according to His will. Tonight as I talked it over with Joe, the man who drove the truck, he said, "We feel it deeply. But the Lord knows what's best. . . ."

Later, when Vonnie received word that her twenty-seven-year-old cousin died suddenly of a cerebral hemorrhage, she found comfort in Joe's words. "It's difficult to understand why my cousin, Bob, was taken," she wrote Walt. "He left a wife and three children. But again I keep telling myself, who are we to question what the Lord allows to happen!"

Vonnie continued to believe the Lord was leading her with regard to Walt and their future. But in August she received another jolt that in her words "crushed" her. She received a letter from Walt that described events at Norman closely resembling her own courtship with him the summer before, only vice versa.

> . . . There's a certain girl here that seems to be pursuing a particular fellow quite persistently. I must confess I've been quite impressed . . . .

The letter offered no further explanation and tore at Vonnie's stomach like a runaway eggbeater. In a subsequent letter Walt told how this same girl always seemed to be next to him during the cafeteria lines and casually mentioned being out with her and holding hands. He did, however, confess that he had not kissed her.

Vonnie responded with, "I'm glad you told me about her. I confess I have mixed feelings. Perhaps I am too tenderhearted." She then told him that she thought he was very mean!

Vonnie's diary indicated she felt terribly helpless, confused, worried, and didn't understand his actions.

Walt wrote an apology in his next letter. "The author of the letter never intended to be mean. It hurts him to know that you were sad. . . ."

Vonnie accepted Walt's apology and for a few lines bathed in elation as he assured her that he still felt no one could be as sweet and lovely as she. But as Vonnie read further, her contented happiness turned to an uneasy feeling of doom.

> As I mentioned before, I have always felt led to work in the South Pacific area and indicated this to the Wycliffe Board when I filled out my application. I must confess, however, since you were in South America that area of the world has become more attractive

to me. I want to know the Lord's will concerning us. I have prayed that if I should get an assignment to your area (without the Board knowing about us) this would be the Lord's indication that we should see more of each other. Since I know how interested you are in Brazil, I thought the Board might assign me there when it opens up. But last Thursday evening, one of the Wycliffe directors told me I was officially assigned to work in Papua, New Guinea. The door is open and Wycliffe must go in while the opportunity is there. There are only fifteen of us going to New Guinea and there is room for fifty translation teams to be allocated within a month.

Since last Thursday I have thought so much about you. And last night I dreamed you were going to the South Pacific with me. I told the director about you and he seemed to think if the Lord had us for each other He would make it plain to you.

Therefore, Vonnie dear, I can only ask you to be mine if the Holy Spirit lays it on your heart to leave Peru and bring you this way.

Thanks for sharing Job 42:2. With Him all things are possible!

Love,

*Walt*

Vonnie's response to Walt's letter was immediate.

August 19

Dear Walter,

I received your letter of August 12 yesterday. I was hesitant to open it because I had the feeling you would be telling me your field assignment. And when I read it, I could hardly believe what I read. It was crushing to my heart. I prayed and was thankful for verses from Psalm 143.

The deepening of my love for you has been very precious to me and the thought of ending our relationship is not easy to look forward to. I know that you want the Lord's will, as I do, and for me this is going to be a heart-searching experience.

If the Lord desires us to be together I know He will show *each* of us. I am also ready to leave Peru and go to the South Pacific if the Lord so desires. I know there would be difficulties. People would raise their eyebrows and tell me I was out of the Lord's will leaving Peru so soon after my arrival. I think my parents will feel this way. But I know the Lord, and know I can do anything He wants me to because His strength and grace are all I need.

I don't know how you feel about me now. Perhaps you think this is the indication we need to show us that we are not meant for each other.

I have grown to love Peru, the base, and my work. I also have a great burden for Brazil. The thought of a new adventure into a difficult situation that means a greater dependence on the Lord is very challenging to my faith. I believe some day in some way the Lord is going to use me for His glory!

Ever since we first started going with each other I have prayed in spite of separation, testing, and waiting, that the Lord would lead us. Even after you told me about this other girl you held hands with, I love you all the more for telling me about it. I hope we will always be able to share everything we do with

each other for I love you very much. Since you shared
this with me I want to share some things with you.

When I received your letter today, I asked the Lord
to help me write from my heart. Before going with
you I had dated only one other fellow (who has since
married). I believed when we were going together
that he loved me. It was wonderful to be loved. No-
body had ever cared or loved me so beautifully before.
But we went out together with our eyes on ourselves,
not on the Lord. Still I loved him and when the Lord
began speaking to me about stressing our physical life
more than our spiritual, I knew I had to break up.
I did, but it was the hardest experience I ever lived
through.

After breaking up I promised the Lord I would be
willing to go anywhere He wanted me to go and I
would go single. I also prayed that if the Lord did have
someone for me it would not be based on physical
attraction but that it would be someone who needed
me so his life could be better used for God's glory.

After meeting you at S.I.L. I felt it was providen-
tial. You know how unusual it was for me to spend
a third summer at Norman. As we started dating
I continually prayed that if we were not meant for
each other the Lord would show you and make it clear.
And even though my love for you has been gradual,
and no one has ever encouraged me, I have a great
peace about our relationship . . . .

Vonnie's letter to Walt and her outside deportment
displayed a clear, brave control of her emotions and feelings. Few if any of her close friends knew or suspected
the deep inner struggles with which she grappled. But

her August 18 diary revealed an unusual level of Christian character and personal grit.

> Saturday, August 18—Received long-awaited letter. Walt assigned to New Guinea. Burden is more than I can bear but nobody must know my feelings. I am beginning a time of fast and prayer.
>
> August 19—Up early for continued prayer. Read Psalm 143. Oh, the Word is such a comfort at this time. This moment is probably the most difficult I'll ever experience.
>
> August 20—A day of heart searching along with being terribly busy. I am conscious of the Lord's strength. Have lost two pounds. The Word is precious. I continue to pray for peace and guidance for the future. I am content that the Lord knows the way through the wilderness.
>
> August 21—Spent time in prayer but weakness keeps me from studying longer. I am praying for a willingness to leave Peru and go with Walt to New Guinea.
>
> August 22—Have mixed feelings. Conscious of Satan's attacks. Dr. Erdman's book, *Storms and Starlight,* a great blessing at this time. I must not ask why but simply trust the Lord completely because I know His way is perfect.

On the twenty-fifth, after a full seven days of fasting, Vonnie made this dramatic notation:

> . . . I have a general sense of weakness but the Lord gives me an abundance of energy to do my work. More than that the Lord has given me my answer. I am

now ready to go to the one I love. Have given over my burden for Brazil to the Lord. Truly the Lord has been good. Had my first drink this afternoon—prune and raisin juice. Felt wonderful all day. The just shall live by faith. I am longing to hear from Walt. Just wrote and told him about my decision.

# 8 _I Love You! I Need You! Will You . . . ?_

It seemed to take forever, but when it came it was as if Vonnie had never waited.

Dearest Vonnie,

Victory! He is giving me peace as I write this. I love you! I need you! Will you be my . . . I mean, will you marry me? Vonnie dear, if you still love me and can answer with the assurance of His peace, please say yes. The Lord has brought me to the place where nothing matters but His will so if you say no or say to wait, I will take it as from Him.

I will wait until I hear from you before I write your folks. Also you should know that I don't have my support yet so you might want to wait until I do.

Vonnie dear, I believe this waiting was necessary to prepare us—to draw us to Him that our home may be honoring to Him. After I finish this I want to pray and ask Him if I should send it right away or wait to see if this is only my feelings. Vonnie, it is wonderful to know that He directs our steps—_that things we can't understand belong to Him._

Tuesday evening
My love, as I was on my knees and looking in His
Word for an answer, He gave me several verses from
James 1, especially verse 5, and Proverbs 4:11, 12. I
have also decided to book passage on the boat for the
two of us. If things don't work out I can always cancel
but thought I would go ahead as reservations have to
be in early.

Love,

*Walt*

P.S. If there is any hesitancy, please *don't* say yes.

There wasn't a moment's hesitancy! The day after Vonnie received Walt's letter, she responded.

My Dearest,
This has been one of the happiest days of my life!
There is much I would like to say but would rather
wait until I see you. I looked back in my diary and
marveled at the way the Lord has led. Forgive me for
all the times I said "Maybe." I am so happy that
you want His will above our own because, when we
do get married, I want our home to be unreservedly
yielded to Him. I am so happy and praise the Lord
for each step of testing and even the waiting which
has been the hardest . . . .

Then with that special kind of feminine mystique that
turns all brides-to-be into a radiant glow of orange sun-
shine, Vonnie's inner soul broke loose. In a torrent of
words that gushed and splattered across eight long pages
and with that singular female ability that has baffled

males since Adam, she repeatedly switched from affection to the mundane. She touched on every subject from a list of kitchen and household needs they would need in New Guinea to warning Walt about how seasick she would become on their honeymoon voyage. She even discussed the practicality of having a wisdom tooth pulled in Peru. "The Doc only charges twenty-five cents—just the cost of the Novocain injection. . . ."

Then after telling Walt how she was going to pack and send her barrels and asking if he thought she should sell her typewriter, she told him not to worry about his support.

> . . . My dearest, I love you and my only desire is to come home as soon as possible to be with you. I am continuing to pray about your support and am confident that the Lord will supply. I remember how the Lord miraculously provided for me to come to Peru and I believe He will provide for you and me to go to New Guinea. Even if you have nothing for your support, it makes absolutely no difference to me. Perhaps through a lack of finances we will learn how to trust Him more. When we get together it will be wonderful to pray about all these little problems. They are nothing to the One who owns the cattle on a thousand hills and holds the stars in place!
>
> I'm so happy that the Lord has worked in ways beyond our understanding. It all seems like a wonderful dream because through the heartbreak of waiting this has become the happiest year of my life. I pray that the Lord might do great things through our lives together. How can we ever doubt His ability to give us the desire of our hearts and provide for our every

need. I want our love for each other to be something beautiful, wonderful, and continually growing. Bye, my dear, until then,

                                        *Vonnie*
Jeremiah 17:5-10

Happiness bubbled like an eternal spring and Vonnie felt as if nothing could ever again cause an anxious moment. But for a few short weeks in November and December, Vonnie and Walt again wondered if the Lord meant them not to marry.

After advising the Peru branch and the Wycliffe Board of her intention to marry, the Peru branch suggested that because they were unable to replace her in the clinic, she might not be able to leave until July or August. The Board then suggested to Walt the possibility of changing his assignment to Peru. Walt's answer to this notion was, "Under no circumstances would I consider a change in assignment. I would rather go to the field single."

After receiving Walt's December 3, 1956, letter outlining his strong convictions about going to New Guinea, Board member Ken Watters forwarded a copy of Walt's letter to Peru's directorship for their response. Director Harold Goodall responded immediately with the following:

Dear Ken,
    Thanks for the letter from Walter Steinkraus. It is helpful to know how he feels about coming to Peru. Evidently he has received the impression that LaVonne may not be transferred. Since they feel the Lord would have them work together, we would not stand in the way of her transfer . . . .

When I first told LaVonne we might not be able to release her until July of '57, she accepted the decision graciously. We, of course, did not know Walter felt so strongly about going to New Guinea. Since then I have discovered that one of our other nurses, who was scheduled to study Spanish, could come as an early replacement and will take her Spanish study at a later date. I also understand that the folks in New Guinea are counting heavily on Walter to come as soon as possible as they are in desperate need of his construction abilities.

In view of all this, we can and will release LaVonne from her Peru assignment. She may leave any time after the first of the year. We have appreciated her work in the clinic but will gladly accept her transfer to New Guinea.

I have asked her to send a prayer letter to her constituency advising them of her new status and reasons for returning to the States after only a year in Peru.

Sincerely in Him,

*Harold Goodall*

There was, however, one final procedure before Vonnie could send out her prayer letter—a letter from Walt to her parents requesting her hand.

Dear Mr. and Mrs. Schreurs,

LaVonne has perhaps already informed you that we are considering going to the mission field together. The Lord led us together during the summer of 1955. We did not think it wise to make any definite plans last year as my training had not been completed. This past summer the Lord indicated New Guinea as the area that He would have me work. This is a high privilege and I am truly grateful to Him for this leading. My heart is already in this land and I can almost see the many tribes there that have been denied God's Message for so long. Please pray for them also.

After receiving this leading I thought that perhaps this was an indication that Vonnie and I were to break up. We both want only the Lord's will always. For only that which is honoring to Him really matters. I was and am still willing to go by myself if this is His will. However, it now appears that He would have Vonnie in New Guinea also. Therefore, I would ask your permission of LaVonne. I shall be very grateful for her, and will strive to be the husband that He would have me be. The Lord in His mercy gave me Christian parents and a home where we had daily family devotions. I praise Him for what this has meant to me. We want our home also to be dedicated to Him where His Word and presence is our daily sustenance.

Sincerely,

*Walter Steinkraus*

Vonnie's parents responded by return mail.

Dear Prospective Son-in-law,

Vonnie has written us regarding a prospective son-in-law, so your letter was not an entire surprise. We know she seeks the Lord's will in this important step in her life, so you being her choice—the Lord's choice —settles everything for Mother and myself. We will feel an extra special blessing in having two of our family in the harvest fields of our Lord instead of one. We pray that our wonderful Lord will continue to guide you in all the steps you take in the future.

The jungles of Peru and New Guinea to me have always seemed so dark and forboding. They seem such a stronghold and domain of the kingdom of darkness. We could wish better things for you both than what this field has to offer in material things. The blessings will have to be spiritual in the knowledge that you serve the Lord, for He is God.

We are acquainted with the fact that you earned your own way through college and other branches of learning and we feel that we certainly can entrust the welfare of our daughter to one who can accomplish this in this busy, tough old world.

If you have time, sometime soon, we would like to have you visit us for as long as you see fit, to discuss any way we may aid you and Vonnie in your plans for the future.

While He tarries we seek to be diligent in business, serving the Lord.

Love,

*Mr. and Mrs. A. J. Schreurs*

Only after this positive response did Vonnie feel free to send out her prayer letter which began with Isaiah 55:8, 9: "For my thoughts are not your thoughts, neither are your ways my ways, saith the Lord. For as the heavens are higher than the earth, so are my ways higher than your ways, and my thoughts than your thoughts."

Dear Friends,

These verses have become increasingly precious to me during recent weeks. Truly, the way the Lord has led is beyond my understanding. I am rejoicing in Him as He has continued to unfold His plan for my life in an unusual and wonderful way. Perhaps many of you will be surprised to hear that after only one year in Peru I am planning to return home to be married to Walter Steinkraus.

I became acquainted with Walter during my last summer of linguistic training. Since then, he, too, has become a member of Wycliffe and completed Jungle Camp and his linguistic studies. Walter is also a graduate of Wheaton College where he majored in Bible. As we have sought the Lord concerning our future the Lord has undertaken in deepening our friendship to one of love and a desire to serve Him together.

We are planning to be married in March and sail for New Guinea on the 6th of April. New Guinea is Wycliffe's newest field. Our first workers will be leaving San Francisco on the 15th of February. The Wycliffe Bible Translators have been challenged by the tremendous task of reaching approximately 700 different language groups in that country.

We covet your prayers that the Lord will fully prepare us for the goal He has set for us, and that in everything He might have preeminence.

Sincerely in Christ,

*Vonnie*

Vonnie wrote her last letter to Walt from Peru on January 25, 1957, twelve days before she was to see him in Chicago. But during a last flight as base nurse, she fully expected never to see Walt again!

Dearest Walt,

Everything has been going wonderfully. My barrels and books are going to Lima next week, the office is taking care of my reservations, and I'll be home soon. Oh, I'm so happy!

Friday night Doc asked me if I would go on the leper flight the next day as the other nurse wanted to leave for Lima. I took my little motion sickness pill but it didn't help. I was sick all day! Yet in spite of this I enjoyed visiting and helping out in the villages. On the way back to base we suddenly flew into a storm and before we knew it we were being tossed around like a puff ball. We had a few anxious moments before the pilot circled and headed for a nearby river. He landed about fifteen minutes before the storm settled in. For awhile before he turned around, it looked as if it might be sudden glory!

Be seeing you soon.

My love always,

*Vonnie*

The boldface capitals on the *Sheboygan Press* society page seemed to breathe a sigh of pleasant relief: **Miss LaVonne Schreurs Is Wed to Walter Steinkraus.** Then followed a two column write-up which told of an unusual wedding trip being enjoyed by a couple wed at 7:30 o'clock Saturday evening at the Evangelical Free Church.

Mr. and Mrs. Walter Steinkraus are en route to San Francisco from where they will sail on April 6 for New Guinea and their new work as missionaries for Wycliffe Bible Translators . . . .

The twenty-three-day voyage from San Francisco to Sydney, Australia, aboard the S.S. *Orion* was all that honeymoon trips are supposed to be. While most of the

tourist passengers in the cramped, overcrowded aft section of the vessel complained about the constant engine
noise, prop vibration, and staterooms without baths,
Walt and Vonnie hardly knew what they were talking
about.

They spent endless hours catching up, sharing and re-
telling the events that led them to their magical hour.
One of these was the way the Lord provided for their
passage. Walt's shy and hesitant speech caused most
churches to bypass him for more "capable" speakers. But
those who worked closely with him knew Walt to be the
man he was. "I will never forget it," said Walt. "One
morning I was spreading gravel with some of the construction crew when all of a sudden they stopped to rest.
I asked them (just kidding) if it was time for lunch.
They said no but that they'd give me five minutes for
a sandwich. Then the bookkeeper took out his checkbook.
I didn't pay too much attention but then he handed me
a check for $595. What a surprise! All I could say was,
'What for?' And then they told me the fellows decided
I could use the money for my passage."

There was, however, an event which they hoped they
could forget! During a short stopover in the Hawaiian
Islands, Walt and Vonnie took a long exploratory hike
in search of native flora. So entranced were they over
the blaze of orchids, brilliant hibiscus, bougainvillea, and
many others, that they failed to hear the ship's whistle
calling them back. Several hours later an annoyed captain stopped his ship in mid-ocean, lowered a rope ladder
onto the deck of an ocean-going tug, and scowled as the
two embarrassed newlyweds clambered aboard to continue on their way.

A shopping tour on a short stopover in Sydney, Australia, ended surprisingly similar to some of Vonnie's early days in Sheboygan. Vonnie noted in her diary:

> Tuesday, April 29—Spent day shopping. Got on wrong trolley and got home quite late!!

The two then boarded an old DC-6 for a long grinding ten-hour flight to Port Moresby, New Guinea's territorial capital. From there they transferred to a smaller aircraft and continued flying north to the port of Lae, New Guinea's gateway to the highlands.

New Guinea, the world's second largest island, is shaped like a wrinkled old man whose beard dips into the Coral Sea and whose pimpled nose juts into the Huon Gulf. It was discovered by the Portuguese in 1511-1512 but named by a Spaniard in 1545 who called the island Papua (Malayan for frizzy hair) and New Guinea because the indigenes resembled those of African Guinea.

Walt had read of savage customs where grieving widows lop off their finger joints with stone axes. And he knew of the unexplored mountain and jungle terrain and the over ten thousand miles of restricted areas where only armed police were allowed to enter. He may not have known, however, about the seventy different species of venomous snakes that crawl through New Guinea's wheatlike kunai grass and tropical rain forests. (The New Guinea death adder and taipan are considered the world's deadliest.) Or the swarms of river crocodiles, insects by the millions, and poisonous stonefish. But Walt didn't choose New Guinea because it wasn't an easy place to live. He chose it because he possessed a sensitive Christ-like concern for people. "I have such a burden (with tears) for the people of New Guinea," he once wrote. And from this burden came a consuming desire to be part of that beginning team which would reach out to the more than five hundred different language groups throughout Papua New Guinea and her surrounding islands.

What began ten years earlier as a budding dream was, on May 1, 1957, both the fulfillment of that dream and the beginning of a new dream. Their first newsletter shared not only a glimpse into their new life but the first hint of their new dream.

. . . Our Ukarumpa Base is in the Aiyura Valley at about five thousand feet. The weather is cool and refreshing, a welcome relief after the terrible heat and humidity of Lae. We can see beautiful mountains in the distance and a swift flowing river bounds our five hundred acres of fertile grasslands. Some years ago this area was the common site for tribal warfare between the Tairora and Gadsup tribes. Isn't it wonderful that it is now being used as a base to reach out to the five hundred language groups with God's Holy Word.

The natives have very dark skin and kinky hair. The women and girls wear skirts made of thin strips of bark saturated with pig's fat. The men wear a wraparound cloth skirt called a *lap lap*. Their diet consists mainly of *pawpaws* or sweet potatoes. These, along with other vegetables and almost no meat, are cooked in an open fire. The men often eat as much as three to seven pounds of vegetables per day!

Their grass and cane homes are oval-shaped and windowless. We are living in a grass hut that will later become the toolshed. They are a very curious folk and one of their main sources of enjoyment seems to be observing us. We often have a crowd standing around the door or peeking in through our windows watching me cook. They are fascinated with all the things we have. It is our prayer that our lives might show forth the love of Christ to them.

Our New Guinea family of Wycliffe workers is growing. We now have nineteen adults and eight children. Two more families and a single girl are due to arrive next month. Yet with all the construction of buildings and preparation of our base, workers are still being assigned to work with the language groups. Two of our single fellows are allocated with the Tairora people and a couple have been assigned to the Fore people.

Since our arrival Walt has been helping with the much needed building program. His electrical training is proving indispensable. We now have five homes and a sawmill in operation. I have been doing some nursing and helping with the base garden. We as yet do not have a tribal location of our own and would ask you to pray for the Lord to lead us to the people of His choice. Pray, too, that our base might grow to become an efficient springboard to all language groups in New Guinea.

Gratefully in Him,

*Walter and Vonnie Steinkraus*

In the months and years that followed, workers from Australia, Canada, Great Britain, New Zealand, the United States, Hong Kong, and South Africa began to swell the

ranks of those who wanted to be involved in Bible translation and supporting roles. The base of operations that
Walt and Vonnie came to in 1957 with less than twenty
people grew to a population of one thousand in 1973—
half Wycliffe workers; half indigenes.

The five small bungalows are still there but have been
surrounded by an additional 170 private dwellings. The
lone sawmill expanded and its neighbors now include a
fire department, post office, primary and high school, radio
department, hangars, auto repair shops, and a sophisticated
battery of technical studies buildings for translation and
linguistic consultation.

The New Guinea base as it stands today grew far beyond
Walt and Vonnie's early expectations, and their quiet
willingness to do whatever was asked of them contributed
significantly to this sturdy growth.

And when the time was right, God led them to a long-
isolated valley close to the West Irian border (formerly
Dutch New Guinea) where from the beginning of time
God purposed they would glorify His name among the
2,800 Tifalmin people.

# 9 Things We Can't Understand

It was the year Boeing's 707 was heralded as the world's fastest, largest, and longest-range jetliner; Berlin was the world's number one trouble spot, Ford's Thunderbird was the "in" car, and crew-cut collegians dated crinoline-swishing coeds. It was 1961, the year after almost four years of waiting that Walt and Vonnie began work among the Tifalmin people in New Guinea's West Sepik district.

They had hoped to work with the neighboring Oksapmin people but government officials kept the area sealed off. Part of their 1960 newsletter, in typical Steinkraus understatements, told some of the reasons for the delay and also some happy, unexpected news.

. . . Last year we had limited contact with two Oksapmin fellows who had come out of the tribe to work at a government station. Their area is still restricted and not considered safe until the government establishes a police post. Just a few years ago two government officers and a native policeman were killed in that area. In the meantime Vonnie and I have been given responsibilities at the base. Vonnie has been helping with the preparation of our New Guinea Handbook and happily caring for our little Kerry Lynn who was born at the Lutheran Mission Hospital on November 21, 1959. She weighed seven pounds, three ounces, and is now very much a part of our family. She's so bright and friendly and her blue eyes and light brown hair make her a favorite among the indigenes. We would ask your prayers in training this little child that she might be a missionary for Him.

I have had the responsibility of erecting the steel frame of the base meetinghouse; also roofing it and laying the cement floor which was all hand-mixed . . . .

In addition to the construction work, Walt and Vonnie assisted Earl and Betty Adams, who had been sent from Mexico to establish a New Guinea Jungle Camp in the famous Markham Valley. Also during this waiting period, Walt, with Alan Pence, former New Guinea Director and Wycliffe's current vice-president of field operations, conducted a month-long language survey for the territorial government. Their survey took them through some of New Guinea's rainiest and roughest country—the steep slippery Owen Stanley Mountains, home of the famed Fuzzy Wuzzy Angels, the indigene stretcher-bearers, who, with uncommon tenderness, compassion, and lung-splitting effort, carried wounded Allied soldiers to safety during World War II.

But it was the kind of adventure Walt loved! Al Pence commented later that although Walt was small, he was just like wire and never seemed to tire. At the end of their long daily hikes Walt always insisted on doing the cooking.

In a small, weather-worn, pocket notebook, Walt recorded some of the events that took place during their month-long hike.

> February 19—Got to top of ridge by noon. The hike from there was very pleasant—a gradual four hour and forty-five minute climb to the village of Kariaritzi. Foot still a little sore. Checked for dialectical pronunciation differences and picked up two short word lists. It started to rain after we arrived. Felt sorry for the six carriers who had to go back over the trail to their village in the lowlands.
>
> February 21—Had cornflake bread and passion fruit for breakfast. Later cooked potatoes and Chinese cabbage. Had Bible study and devotions with Al— Ephesians 2 and 3. This was a great blessing to us. Left Kariaritzi for Kerau. Rained most of way. Elevation 7,000 feet. Had good time finding out about the customs of the people. Chief's influence is still very strong. They tried to keep his identity secret by working through a spokesman. But when a decision had to be made, the chief nodded to his spokesman. At night we sat around the campfire and talked.
>
> February 26—Had two cornflake bread for breakfast. Almost two hours to next village. Paid two shillings for each carrier. After we arrived the carriers refused to go on. Suggested to Al he go to Guari for help. I stayed back with gear and got to work getting word lists on tape recorder. Was surprised to find only one woman with about fourteen men. Washed a few things out in stream.

March 2—People of village tried to discourage us from
going on, saying it was the wrong time of year to
climb over the high ridge. They said five of their
men died when they tried. We gave the carriers rain
hoods and they seemed willing to go. (Found out
later they were from a different area.) Our climb
was immensely steep and hard going. The forest
was thick and a cold drizzly rain fell as we gained
elevation. The wind blew in mist that fogged up
glasses and numbed fingers. Stopped about 12:30
and built fire in small native bark shelter. Shared
lunch of cornflake bread with carriers. Then
started down ahead of carriers. Strong winds from
behind. Grass most of way. Arrived in village at
3:00. They told about a mission house at Garoha.
It seemed a long way but pushed on through a
thick bush trail. Arrived at 5:05. The mission house
was nice but I was so tired I felt like crying.
Couldn't eat much. Mostly soup. Al did all right.

March 3—Up at 7:00. Good breakfast of potatoes, cab-
bage soup, and raisins . . . .

March 5—Got an early start—about 7:20. Bush trail for
most of way. Left knee started to bother me. Put
on Al's knee band which helped. The climb in most
places was gradual. Crossed over a river and had
trouble with strong gusty winds. Al's face red at
times and had to brace ourselves and catch our
breath. We found it more difficult as we neared
summit. Arrived about 11:30 A.M. Had to wait
about fifteen minutes in the rain for the carriers.
They didn't want a fire so ate cold baked potatoes,
tomatoes, and raisins. After lunch continued along
summit. It rained and wind was gusty and cold.
Could do with some mittens. Arrived at village

about 3:00. People very excited. Men and women
came out to shake our hands. We left sixteen shill-
ings for carriers and left message for new carriers
to bring gear on to police post at Guari. We arrived
there about 5:30 and into bed about 6:30. Praise
the Lord—a wire from Vonnie! Miss Vonnie and
Kerry very much.

Several months after this grueling hike, the government administrative personnel that favored opening the
door to the Oksapmin area changed. Their replacements
felt the area should remain closed for an indefinite period
of time. On the suggestion of fellow worker Alan Healey,
and at the encouragement of the Baptist mission to begin
a translation program in the area, Walt and Vonnie prayed
and felt led to work with the Tifalmin people.

According to reports, government patrols opened up the
country in the mid-fifties and promptly forbade the practice of intertribal warfare, cannibalism, and the practice
of putting their dead in trees. Nevertheless, when Walt
and Vonnie arrived to work among the Tifalmin people,
the government restricted their movements to within a
mile radius of the Baptist mission airstrip.

But no matter how complete the reports, nothing fully
prepared Walt and Vonnie for living day after day with
people who for centuries have had their spirits caged and
controlled by Satan. The difference in culture, language,
dress, and eating habits paled beside the sudden and awful
realization that they were entering into Satan's domain.

At first this did not dominate their thoughts. They con-
centrated on hearing the Tifal language and identifying
with the people. In September 1961 Walt wrote: "In recent

weeks the language is becoming more than just an accumulation of unfamiliar sounds. We are beginning to understand a little of the language structure and look forward to the day when we will be able to talk to them about spiritual things in their own language. . . ."

Then as Walt and Vonnie developed a sensitivity to the needs of the Tifalmin people, they realized people at home could assist them in the battle against their common enemy. Walt wrote in a special request-for-prayer bulletin:

In the brief time we have been here, we have seen and felt the tragic effects of people in the grip of satanic superstition. Last Sunday we ate supper with three of the native girls. It was a lovely evening; the girls giggled and chatted as we sat on an old log by the river and roasted corn. Then one of the girls, Unagin, washed out her gourd water bottle, smiled at us, and walked away into the night. A short time later as we returned to our small house, we suddenly heard terrible screams. In a moment several men with tortured looks of horror on their faces ran down the trail into the jungle. In a few moments they returned carrying Unagin, unconscious but alive. When we asked what happened they told us she tried to hang herself. We were speechless. Why would this seemingly carefree girl who had just left us try to kill herself? The next day we learned why. She had quarreled with her husband and wanted to join her girl friend, who, five days earlier, hung herself because she was unhappy over the man her family had chosen for her to marry.

We are also concerned over the decreasing Tifalmin population. The death wail is becoming more and more frequent. Sometimes it's a child or older person who has died. But often it is a young mother or father who died because a sorcerer told them an ancestral ghost was causing their sickness and they would never get better. And they didn't!

Believing the One whom they served would prevail, and trusting a promise from Exodus 23:20, Walt and Vonnie continued to make friends, treat the sick, and explain why they had come to live in Tifalmin. The high mortality rate, they discovered, came from the area's most devastating sickness—malaria—plus tropical ulcers, pneumonia, and infected bush-knife cuts. Although a few immediately accepted them, many showed cold indifference until Vonnie won their confidence when she attended the headman's wife during childbirth complications.

Walt slowly gained friends and respect by growing and sharing what he knew about gardening, asking the people for tips on how they grew their gardens, and by going out once a week to hunt with the young men of the village. "Besides sharing in the kill," said Walt, "this is an excellent way to gain fluency in the language."

And because they knew how to plod and make friends in the face of initial indifference, in December 1962, after eight long months with the Tifalmin people, they were able to write:

Suyeng and Kogon, two of our dear friends and among the first Tifalmin couples to express their desire to become Christians, have been experiencing deep spiritual battles. They were the first to welcome us to the tribe and have encouraged us with their friendliness and help in learning the Tifalmin lan-

guage. Last October Kogon become critically ill after
the birth of their second child. We prayed that God
would spare her life and God did answer our prayers
but saw fit to allow her child to die several weeks
later. It is hard for us to try and explain about the
sovereignty of God.

As we have seen God at work we have also seen
the forces of the evil one at work. There have been
numerous tribal quarrels and family feuds. Stealing
and lying are the common practice of many and the
fear of sorcery and evil spirits is always present. Recently one of the men from upper Tifalmin died after
a short illness. The headman explained that the spirit
man shot him with an arrow and quickly broke off
the arrow so no one could see where the arrow pene-
trated his body.

A baby boy died in our village two days after we
started treating him for malaria and diarrhea. The
child was anemic and dehydated but his parents objected to us treating him because they said an evil
spirit had entered his body and there was no hope
of his recovery.

After the child died, the people of the village
mourned and feasted for several days. During this
time the child's brokenhearted father was rescued
twice from attempting suicide by hanging himself.

Since coming to Tifalmin we have come to understand the meaning of Ephesians 6:12 that we wrestle
not against flesh and blood but against the one who
fights to maintain control over those who have been
under his dominion for so long.

There was a further note at the end of this prayer and
newsletter that said they planned to be in Tifalmin for

three more months and then fly home for furlough. But in April, even though they had not seen their families for five years, Walt and Vonnie postponed their furlough for a year—first to take advantage of a special series of language workshops conducted by Dr. Kenneth Pike, and second, because they felt the extended time with the Tifalmin people would cement relations and give them greater facility in the language.

But one morning, shortly after their return to Tifalmin after attending the language workshop, Jim Baptista, chief pilot for Wycliffe's New Guinea JAARS program, logged the following report:

> The first inkling of an emergency came when Walt radioed the base for a flight. He said Vonnie was extremely ill and after describing her symptoms it seemed almost certain to be cerebral malaria. We clearly had to get them out fast. But the weather report from their area was bad. Since the flight would take over two hours, I decided to go ahead and pray that by the time I arrived the weather would be clear enough to land.
>
> I refueled at Mt. Hagen, the half-way point, to maximum capacity and called the control tower in Madang for the latest weather report. It was bad. But I knew weather in New Guinea could change quickly and decided to continue. After flying for an hour in perfect conditions, the lowering overcast and rising mountain ridge suddenly met five minutes before I was to reach my destination. I then flew along the ridge looking for a break in the clouds but could find none.
>
> The only thing left for me to do was turn back to

where the overcast began and try to go over the top.
I thought I might find a hole in the clouds over their
valley. I retraced my course for twenty-five minutes
and climbed to 16,500 feet. It was clear. I then noted
the time and took a compass reading and after flying
for twenty minutes I calculated my position as being
over Telefomin which is about six minutes flying time
from Tifalmin. It was now 12:15 P.M. and I called
Madang for the noon weather report. "Eight hundred
foot overcast, visibility two miles in moderate rain."
It seemed unlikely that the weather would be any
different at Tifalmin but I committed the situation to
the Lord. I knew the folks back at the base were also
praying.

After another five minutes I calculated my position
as being over Tifalmin but couldn't be sure as I
hadn't seen the ground and knew the wind could have
blown me off course. Just as I was considering turning
around and heading for home, I saw a break in the
clouds. A closer examination revealed the hole to be
directly over Tifalmin! I reduced speed, lowered flaps,
and started down in a very steep turn—from 16,500
to 4,500 feet. I landed, dizzy, but full of thanks to the
Lord.

Walt and I quickly closed up their house, carried
Vonnie to the plane and made her comfortable on the
floor. Walt held Kerry Lynn and I fitted the rest of
their things where I could find space. I told Walt
about the bad weather and said it would be impossible to climb up through the hole I had just come
down. This meant the only way out was the way I
had tried to come in earlier.

As we flew out of the valley I looked in the direction of the Telefomin airstrip and saw the rain and

clouds that had been reported. The only part of the valley that was open was the end where Walt and Vonnie lived. As we approached the ridge where I had been turned back earlier (this time from the opposite side), the clouds looked just the same as they had an hour and a half before.

I flew alongside the ridge looking for a hole and again asked the Lord to open the clouds. Suddenly a small hole appeared and I was able to see through to the other side. Circling around, I crossed the ridge and flew back to the base without a hitch.

Two days later Walt scribbled a note to Vonnie's parents.

Dear Mother and Dad,

I am writing this from the hospital. Yesterday I sent you a wire asking prayer for Vonnie and now the Lord has put His hand upon her and answered our prayers even before we asked. She is still weak but has definitely improved since yesterday. Vonnie became sick about twelve days ago, first with pains in her legs, then fever and severe headaches. At first we thought it was a reaction to a cholera shot. Then on Friday the Baptist mission plane came in with some visitors and Vonnie got up to entertain them.

On Saturday she was worse—no appetite, high temperature, unable to sleep, severe headache, and very thirsty. The symptoms were much like cerebral malaria and she took treatment for this. Her temperature gradually came down after she took the pills but in a few hours it came back again. On Sunday she began to have pain in her kidneys and began not to function properly. We knew that if her kidneys stopped functioning she would not pull through as this was one of the symptoms that brought about the death of one of the natives here.

We had a time of earnest prayer and asked the Lord to relieve the pressure and in a short while her kidneys began to improve. On Monday we called the base and asked for prayer. Vonnie thought she was too weak for a plane trip to the base. However, as the fever hung on and she wasn't able to sleep, we felt the Lord would have us call for the plane on Tuesday morning.

The weather was bad but the Lord opened a hole in the clouds near our airstrip and the plane got through. How thankful we are for radio and plane service! The trip was painful for her and she wasn't able to get much rest that night. In the morning she was nearing coma stage from exhaustion. As soon as the fog lifted we took off for the hospital in Madang. The weather was good and we had a smooth trip. She is now under the care of Dr. Brown, a competent physician. He gave her intravenous feedings as she was dehydrated, and took tests. She was able to rest today and her temperature has come down to normal. She is being treated for kidney infection but it appears no surgery is required. We are praying for her complete recovery.

This experience has been a time of searching our hearts and has drawn us closer to the Lord. It has also given us fellowship together in prayer such as we have never known before.

We have had to say good-bye to our Tifalmin friends and were not able to get the things done we had hoped to before leaving for furlough. But the Lord has taught us that *complete commitment* to Him is more important than our *service*.

With love,

*Walt*

However, in the years that followed their 1963-64 furlough, Walt and Vonnie's complete commitment to Christ meant service—service to the Tifalmin people as they gave them the tools to develop a growing church—translated Scriptures and hymns in their own language.

And they gave service to the base where their modest but efficient bungalow by the river became the flower and garden show place of Ukarumpa and whose door was open to people in the true manner of Romans 12:9-13. They didn't just pretend to love people but took honest delight in honoring their contemporaries. The people brought home for dinner were often the quiet, shy, forgotten, and overlooked.

Their commitment meant maintaining a perennial freshness for Bible translation and a sense of urgency in reaching the language groups of New Guinea. "It's good to be here at the base," Walt once wrote, "to fellowship with our friends and meet the new Wycliffe workers. The Lord has been good to us in sending wonderful people to do Bible translation but there are still many more needed if we are to reach all the tribes."

It meant maintaining a growing love relationship in their marriage. Few if any of their friends ever saw Walt display his affection for Vonnie. Yet it was plain for all to see as was his deep affection for Kerry Lynn and later little Kathryn who was born in 1968.

In a letter as written by Kerry Lynn to her cousins, Vonnie wrote:

. . . My name is Kerry Lynn. I am three years old and a little more. I have blond hair and blue eyes and Mommy and Daddy think I am very pretty.

I have gone through a hard time as Mommy and my Teddy were sick. During that time Daddy was awfully good to me. He pulled me in my red wagon, read me stories, and pushed me in the swing. Mommy wasn't able to cook so Daddy cooked for me. Sometimes he made me special things like apple pies. I always love Daddy to read to me. My favorite stories are about Bill and Jerry at school and Bambi.

I spent a lot of time playing with my little Tifalmin friends. Taugan is a little girl like me and my size. Her daddy tried to hang himself when her baby brother died. We were all very sad.

Sometimes I get naughty and Daddy spanks me real hard. One time I tried to help Daddy catch baby chicks. They wouldn't stop so I hit one with a piece of bamboo. It almost stopped and Daddy spanked me. I cried awfully hard. I went to Mommy and said, "Mommy, I just want to be a flower in the grass." Mommy said she didn't want me to be a flower in the grass because I was their little sweetheart and they loved me too much. I thought that was a nice thing to say . . . .

Commitment to Christ for Vonnie and Walt was a responsibility to the Christian community at large. Out of their $301.67 monthly support in 1967 that came from friends and two small churches, they gave financial help to Wycliffe projects outside New Guinea and not only supported long-admired Billy Graham, but came to his defense when a radio preacher blasted Graham in his magazine for appearing on "Laugh In."

Dear Mr. ———:

I am writing in reference to an article which appeared in your magazine entitled, "Graham Brings Jokes to

'Laugh In.' " An attack of this nature on a fellow servant of the Lord can only be understood as a hindrance to the cause of Christ. Our Lord solemnly warned us against judging others in Matthew 7:1-5. I would humbly ask you to prayerfully seek His guidance before allowing an article of this nature to appear in your publication.

A Reader

*Walter Steinkraus*

For Walt commitment also meant a willingness to accept his mother's death in January 1968. In a letter to Edna and Marge he wrote, "Mother has had a long and useful life and has faced many hardships. We are happy she has been called home . . . ."

Total commitment meant accepting themselves as God made them, even with what some of their colleagues considered strange idiosyncrasies. "We always braced ourselves when the Steinkrauses either came or went to the tribe," said flight coordinator, John Sahlin. Walt's January 11, 1969, letter to his sister explained why. "We moved back to the tribe. *We* includes the whole family—five ducks, eight hens, one rooster, a dog, and two cats. The hens keep us well supplied with eggs, the cats keep the rats away, and the dog doesn't have much to do but the people think he is rather special and important."

And their commitment meant not living in a vacuum. When their second furlough of 1969-70 arrived after years of isolation from America's ills, Walt and Vonnie showed genuine concern over the nation's strange new turbulence. Anecdotes for Vonnie's messages came from *Time, News-*

*week,* and Tom Skinner, the energetic Black evangelical spokesman.

"The problems of civil rights, drugs, and excessive permissiveness are different only in make-up from the problems found in New Guinea," said Vonnie. "Whether man lives in a sophisticated or primitive society his basic problem is living independently from God. And this is sin!

"This is why we believe Bible translation is so important. Because the elements that bring about effective character and attitude change come only through a knowledge of God through His Son, Jesus Christ. And the translated Scriptures are essential to this change."

Happily, their 1969-70 furlough was not all an intense struggle with current issues. Walt studied Hebrew at Wheaton and after fifteen years of watching Vonnie play tennis, finally learned to thwack a sizzler across the net.

There was time to frolic in the Wisconsin snow and take Kerry Lynn skiing. And afterward there was the warmth of the Schreurs's home—a time to sit around an old-fashioned oak table in the living room and snack on crackers and cheese cut from a two-pound block of Gibbsville Wisconsin cheddar. A time for grandparents to romp with their grandchildren and Kerry Lynn to tell Grandma and Grampa about New Guinea beetles that tasted like burnt chocolate when you roasted them. A time to take a son-in-law ice fishing and for sisters to reminisce about Volrath Park, North Point Beach, and Grampa's farm. A time to sleep in a poster bed with eiderdown quilts and a time to shop at Prang's Department Store. In all, their time at home was a cozy experience, like being by a warm fire on a cold night. And when they returned to New Guinea in mid-1970, friends and parents wept.

While Vonnie and Walt felt the heavy sting of farewell tears, it was only for a moment. Because while it was difficult to say good-bye, it would have been harder not to return to New Guinea and the Tifalmin people. "We know as clearly as we know our own names," said Walt, "that God wants us in New Guinea!"

Like most missionary parents, Walt and Vonnie faced the problem of children's schooling. "After we returned," wrote Walt, "I went out to the village for two weeks to see the people and bring back a couple of fellows to work on translation. We wanted to go out as a family but Kerry's school principal suggested she finish out her sixth grade at the base school. We are doing this and remaining with her until the end of the school year which in New Guinea is the end of December.

"One of the first things I plan to do when we go out in January is put a galvanized roof on our house. I discovered it was leaking again . . . ."

When the whole family did return on January 15, 1971, Walt began immediately to sandwich house and garden repair between Bible translation. In one of his last letters dated February 25, 1971, Walt wrote:

We were impressed with the ministry of a visiting Pastor Riffel who spoke at the base the Sunday before we left for Tifalmin. He will be conducting a series of informal lectures and Vonnie would like to go back to the base in March to get in on some of these. She thinks they might help us in dealing with some of the problems we are having in the Tifalmin church. The more we translate the Scriptures, the more Satan seems to attack the believers.

Kerry and Kathy are happy here and love to play outdoors with their friends. Kerry's correspondence lessons have not arrived yet but we brought some books from the base school and Vonnie helps her with these. I think Kerry would rather teach than do her own schoolwork. She has what she calls her literacy class for some of her friends and is actually teaching them to read and write. She also has children's church each Sunday morning. These are her own ideas and of course we are pleased to see her take such an active and helpful interest in the work. We got her a sewing machine for Christmas as she likes to sew. It's a lovely hand-crank Chinese model (paid $27.50) and now Kerry is making skirts (with Von's help) and sells them to the girls and women of the village . . . .

Vonnie did return to the base at Ukarumpa. She listened to Pastor Riffel's lectures and was spiritually encouraged. Before returning to the village she took one last exhilarating canter around the government agricultural station with eighteen-year-old Linda Hunt. To her and others Vonnie expressed their love for the Tifalmin people and how much they felt at home with them. "But," said Vonnie, "Satan seems to have many of them in his grip." And then she asked for prayer that the Lord would do something special to break Satan's hold.

Later, as she waited for the dull blue carryall to pick her up from the hilltop Ukarumpa guest house and take her to the airstrip, the base hostess asked her how long she planned to remain in the village. "I don't know," replied Vonnie, "but I feel the whole family should stay there. We need to be there to glorify God as a family."

As the sleek twin-engine Aztec soared out of the Aiyura valley and headed for Tifalmin, Vonnie popped a motion-sickness pill into her mouth and settled back to think about Walt and the children. Walt's March 15 radio call on their fourteenth wedding anniversary was still fresh in her memory.

"Congratulations on the successful completion of fourteen years of marriage. May all these years of shared blessings and happiness return as cherished memories today. Love, *Walt, Kerry, Kathy.*"

These truly had been happy years and it reminded her of a letter she had written to Walt after she accepted his proposal of marriage.

My Dearest Walter,

I love you as much as ever I can. My prayer and great desire for both of us is to be the woman and man God wants us to be. I pray that we will never fail Him, He who has done so much for us.

When I think of this, John 12:24 keeps coming into my mind: "Verily, verily, I say unto you, Except a corn of wheat fall into the ground and die, it abideth alone: but if it die, it bringeth forth much fruit . . . ."

It was Friday, March 19, 1971 . . . .

# *10*  *Reflections*

On Sunday, March 21, at 3:00 P.M., two days after her return, Walt, Vonnie, eleven-year-old Kerry Lynn, and two-year-old Kathy died—buried in their village by a landslide.

Two eyewitnesses ran three miles to a mining camp and reported the disaster. Wycliffe personnel arrived on Monday and pieced together the following report:

The weather was bright and peaceful. Walt, Vonnie, and the family attended church in a nearby village Sunday morning. Because the weather was so perfect, most villagers were outside the village working in their gardens or gathering firewood. Only seven people besides the Steinkraus family were in the village. Walt and Vonnie were either resting or asleep. Then at 3:00 P.M. a huge section of a three-hundred-foot mountain on the opposite side of the river from the Steinkraus's house broke loose. There was a terrible roar as with incredible force the half-mile-wide, one-hundred-foot-deep section scooped out sandbanks, crossed the river, and drove through to the opposite bank covering the village with ten feet of rock, mud, and debris. Death was instantaneous.

In the days that followed, memorial services were held in New Guinea, Sheboygan, Madison, and Chicago. Understandably, friends and family were stunned. Many asked *why?* When objectivity returned, some reflected.

"I was just getting out of my car," said Gil Dodds, "when I heard the news over WMBI in Chicago. I sat there stunned for a moment, then thanked God for the privilege of knowing Wally." Later at a memorial service in Chicago, Gil said, "Wally was a guy who was always reaching out and chose Wycliffe because it had the challenge he wanted. His work on earth was brief compared to all his preparation for service, but I believe his work was completed. If it wasn't God wouldn't have called him home."

Walt's brother, Sam, agreed with Gil's last statement and added, "Odd as it may seem, I thought how wonderful for the whole family to be ushered into heaven together."

In a letter, Walt's sister, Mrs. Marge Garver, wrote:

I thank God I have so many happy memories of my brother, Walter. He was a year and a half younger than I and we grew up sharing many of the same thoughts and dreams. When he was still in grade school, three boys rubbed his gums with a cigarette until they bled. They wanted to make him smoke. I was disgusted and wanted to get even with them. But Walt just laughed and said, "Marge, we will just pray for them; they didn't mean any harm. They just didn't know any better." And after that they really respected Walt.

When we were expecting our second child I prayed it would be a boy that would look like my husband and have Walt's patience and good nature. And God answered my prayer!

When our first child, Brenda, was born, Walt spent a month with us and enjoyed her so much. He told me then that he probably would never have the joy of a family as he felt it would be unfair to a girl to ask her to share a life of hardship living in a tribe. That, of course, was before he met Vonnie. Walt didn't know God was already preparing a wife for him. When I first met Vonnie I felt she was one of God's choicest gems. And as time went on she became so dear to me. It was a privilege just knowing her. She was a wonderful wife to Walt and a good mother to Kerry and Kathy. If they had to go so soon, I'm thankful they could all go together. Only our heavenly Father knows why . . . .

Walt's youngest sister, Mrs. Violet Seebold, shared that Walt never said a cross word to her or anyone, but was always kind and considerate even as a child. "How well I remember him milking the cows and doing all the other chores that go with it before going off to school in the morning. He never complained but was always very cheerful and at times amusing as he had a good sense of humor. He knew how to handle Mama who was not only strict but a bit eccentric at times. He could deal with her better than any of the rest of us. Like the time he played football. She objected, but he assured her all was going to be fine. Well, one day he came home with two black eyes and didn't see how he could face Mama. So he got a pair of sunglasses and wore them indoors and out. But she chose that day to cut his hair!

"Her worries about Walt getting hurt were not all in vain as one day he developed blood poisoning in his leg due to a football injury. He didn't want to tell her about it but in the middle of the night it became so painful he had to. We lived six miles from a doctor and didn't have a telephone or car. My invalid father couldn't be of much assistance so it was up to Mama and her strong faith—along with Walt's! As always, God undertook. Mama recalled a simple home remedy and Walt came out of it beautifully . . . ."

Walt's older sister, Mrs. Edna Gertz, remembers that she and her sisters went over to a neighbor's for the day while a midwife delivered Walter. "What a treat to come home to find a baby brother, after five sisters!

"When Walt was a year old my sisters and I decided to find out what he was going to be when he grew up. We put a number of things on the table to see what he would choose—a writing tablet (writer), twigs (forester), ball (ballplayer), grain and corn (farmer), Bible (preacher or missionary), pieces of cloth (manufacturer), tools (carpenter). When we sat him down in the midst of these items, he chose the Bible. Even as youngsters we strongly believed he would be a missionary or preacher so it wasn't a surprise when he went to Wheaton and Bible school. It was just as if this was what he was supposed to do . . . ."

"For some reason," said Phyllis Meier, Vonnie's sister who lives in Madison, Wisconsin, "I was praying for Pastor Mooney and the work in Sheboygan that morning. So when Pastor Mooney called I wasn't surprised. But when he told me, I felt like a tornado hit me. I don't suppose I'll ever again experience such grief. I didn't question it. I know the Lord doesn't make mistakes—He does all things well. In a mighty way, even though everything on the outside was horrible, the Lord's presence inside was unusually warm and comforting. And because He knew I needed it, the Lord brought my husband home unexpectedly at noon, something he never does.

"When I called home, my daddy said, 'Your little mama can't talk right now.' I asked him if I should come home but he said with almost a whisper, 'No, let's see how this is going to work out. We'll call again tomorrow.' The next day they drove up and Daddy said, 'You know we just had to come. You're all we've got now.'"

Pastor Ellis M. Mooney of the Evangelical Free Church in Sheboygan, Wisconsin, broke the news to Vonnie's parents. And in the days that followed he reflected: "What does a pastor reflect upon when he receives word that an outstanding missionary family of his congregation have given their lives on the front lines of Christian service? The first impression is one of disbelief—there must be a mistake. This is followed by the shock of reality and love; then tears flow freely, intermittently throughout the day. Not tears of grief, but tears for the immediate family —tears of personal loss of dear friends—even tears of joy for their terminal safety.

"Interested folk call to confirm the story, and speak of the tragedy of death. But deep inside I cannot call it a tragedy, nor even a disappointment. Rather it was a divine appointment and a moment of triumph. But will those to whom you speak have the same glorious faith in Christ? Will they understand the truth of death as taught in Scripture? Possibly not. Yet it is that faith in *truth* which brings meaning and fulfillment to an hour such as this. 'To be absent from the body is to be present with the Lord' [*see* 2 Corinthians 5:8]. 'For to me to live is Christ, and to die is gain . . . to be with Christ; which is far better' [Philippians 1:21, 23]. This is reality. Our friends are in His presence—they are enjoying something far better. This is triumph! They knew Jesus Christ personally—and to know Him is life eternal.

"After a bit the memory thumbs through the pages of the past. Little things take on a new perspective. How lovely and refreshing those memories can be. As a girl, Vonnie loved the out-of-doors, the world of flowers and clover, and the training of her dog. So it was not strange to have her write after reaching Jungle Camp, 'I just love the jungle.' During one week of her younger life she was kicked by a cow, hit by a car, and bit by a dog! Yet she wasn't injured. Nothing seemed to bother her except motion sickness.

"Vonnie was a college freshman when she came to know Jesus Christ personally, made a complete commitment to Him, and found out how wonderful it really was to be a Christian. From that time on she felt strongly that she was to be a missionary. But more than that, she first and foremost wanted to be a genuine Christian woman.

"One incident of particular interest involved her engagement to Walter. Vonnie had gone to Peru with Wycliffe and while there, Walter, whom she had met earlier, began corresponding with her. Regarding this growing romance she wrote: 'Walter has asked me to join him in the work in New Guinea . . . . I love him very much and feel that this is of the Lord. Yet we know that when two people are in love our hearts can betray us . . . . As

my pastor I know you have been praying for God's guidance in my life and I know you are interested in my problem. Perhaps you would like to see Walter . . . .' So
Mrs. Mooney and I arranged to meet Walter, evaluate
the man, and give our approval. Sometimes the pastor is
called to be Cupid's associate!

"And what was Walter like? A quiet fellow, slow of
speech, and full of energy. His abilities did not appear
on the surface. But underneath there was a rare and mag-
nificent man. He had a fine mind and a deep love for
the Lord. He found time to be a track star and was one
of the top cross-country runners of the collegiate world.
He chose to run barefoot whenever the rules did not
forbid.

"A few years later he would lead the tribesmen on
long, cross-country mountainous survey treks. They might
tire—Walt would not. Vonnie was the public speaker of
the family; Walt was the linguist.

"While home this past year he laid sod, built fences,
and helped to construct rock walls for the Youth Center's
recreational area in his spare time. He went out on visita-
tion work and formulated a complete program of missionary education for use throughout the Sunday school and
church. Walter never sought any recognition—only an
opportunity to work.

"I am convinced the servants of the Lord are inde-
structible until their work is done. Therefore I believe
that Walter and LaVonne had completed their assignment.
They left behind as a memorial of their own, the greatest
Book in the world—the New Testament, in part, in the
Tifal language, and twelve years of linguistic work."

(A new Wycliffe translation team was assigned to the

Tifalmin in 1972, and because Walt and Vonnie carefully preserved duplicate copies of their language data in Ukarumpa, began with a twelve-year head start!)

"Walter and LaVonne Steinkraus, Kerry Lynn and Kathy, received a directive from their Heavenly Headquarters calling them into immediate service in the Home Office. They had served their term as Ambassadors to New Guinea 'in Christ's stead,' and discharged their duties honorably. In the providence of God they had completed their term of field duty and their General Director transferred them to permanent furlough in the Gloryland."

Gladys Strange remembers when they first arrived at the base in New Guinea after their honeymoon voyage. "Everyone on the base welcomed them. There were few houses then—two big thatch and bamboo houses, one smaller thatch, one iron-roofed house and a thatch garage. Walt and Vonnie got the eight-by-ten-foot workroom at the back of the garage. When it rained hard the rain filtered through the thin thatch roof onto the dirt floor. But at all times they maintained their 'honeymoon' cheerfulness.

"It didn't take long for Vonnie's love of gardening to show up and they had the first good lawn with beautiful flowering borders. They ordered fruit trees along with their first grocery order. To ease the burden of his workers, Walt built the first wheelbarrow with a handmade wooden wheel . . . ."

Adrian Verschure, Australian New Guinea branch member, recalled how he first came to know Walt while working on the construction of a difficult airstrip north of

Tifalmin. "Before working with Walt I knew him as a linguist and translator but during the three weeks with him I came to know him as a Christian gentleman, a quiet and confident worker of the Lord, and a loving husband and father. Even in the pouring rain, mud, and slush, felling heavy trees, dealing with primitive people, he never lost his patience and always displayed the spirit of his Lord. In his quiet and humble way he inspired all to give their best and, in spite of difficult conditions, the job was done in record time. He may not have translated as many parts of the New Testament as other members, but to me, and all others working with him on that rugged job, he translated the whole gospel of his Lord by demonstration and example. We rejoice that now he and his loved ones have received their due reward for faithful service to our heavenly Master."

The memory of Walt and Vonnie for James Dean, former New Guinea director, is that of commitment to the task of Bible translation. "I remember their freshness and fullness of joy as they began their overseas service for the Lord. Their fine riverside home at Ukarumpa, while lacking in extravagance, set a standard of excellence in workmanship that was a guide for many to follow. Their beautiful garden showed their love for growing things and they contributed greatly to the inspiration for fine group gardens at Ukarumpa. The beauty of floral arrangements at weddings and other functions often reflected the skillful and loving attention of Vonnie, and her love of riding and skill with horses enabled her to inspire many of our children to ride.

"Walt showed special interest in the skills of Bible translating from the earliest days. That was why he was suggested to attend John Beekman's workshop in Mexico. As a member of the Translation Department, he contributed much to the excellence of others' translations as well as his own.

"In the little village of Tifalmin, Walt and Vonnie were happy to live their lives for their Lord, allowing His love to flow through them to those people. Years ago when I visited them in their village home I was impressed with the wonderful way they identified with the Tifalmins. They were living among them and their lives had become intermingled with theirs. Their ideas of organic gardening, cleanliness, and health, as well as their quiet faith and love in the Lord, flowed out and affected the Tifalmins.

"Why should they be taken in a tragic landslide? Why does a gardener pluck some of the most beautiful blooms —even at times with choice buds to enhance them?

"At least we can be assured that the Creator of the whole universe certainly allowed it, and in some way unknown to us at this time it will bring glory to His Name. 'Greater love hath no man than this, that a man lay down his life for his friends.'"

And a father-in-law wrote his own tribute to his son-in-law:

. . . Sometimes when tragedy strikes, we ask, *why?* We forget that we are the clay and our Lord the Potter. It is not for the clay to demand, "What doest thou?" Job had the right answer: "The Lord gave, and the Lord hath taken away; blessed be the name of the Lord" [Job 1:21].

Few men have worked harder as missionaries than

Walter. When they arrived at the mission field there were few buildings at the base. He built his own home, and a nice one, from standing trees. He dragged the trunks across the river with a jeep. He helped to build and supervised the building of some of the main buildings on the base. As a reward for this industry he stayed an extra year before furlough because he had spent an extra year in building when he had been sent as a translator.

He traveled many miles on foot in survey work to establish other translators in other tribes. He helped to build airstrips with ax and crowbar. This was done in addition to his first love, which was translation work, so that a people known as the Tifalmin might for the first time hear of the wonderful grace of God in their own language.

When we ask, "Why was he taken from his work which was still not completed?" I feel the answer to be this: Our Lord said, "Walter, you have labored so hard all your days that I am going to let your work for others be finished. I am going to take you home. You have loved your family so dearly, and they have been so close to you and have loved you so much, that I want you to stay together and all come home to Me together that where I am you may be also."

Maybe that is not exactly the way it was, but I like to think it was that way.

As for Mother and me, we agree with Job. Our Lord gave and our Lord has taken away. BLESSED BE THE NAME OF THE LORD.

*Dad Schreurs*